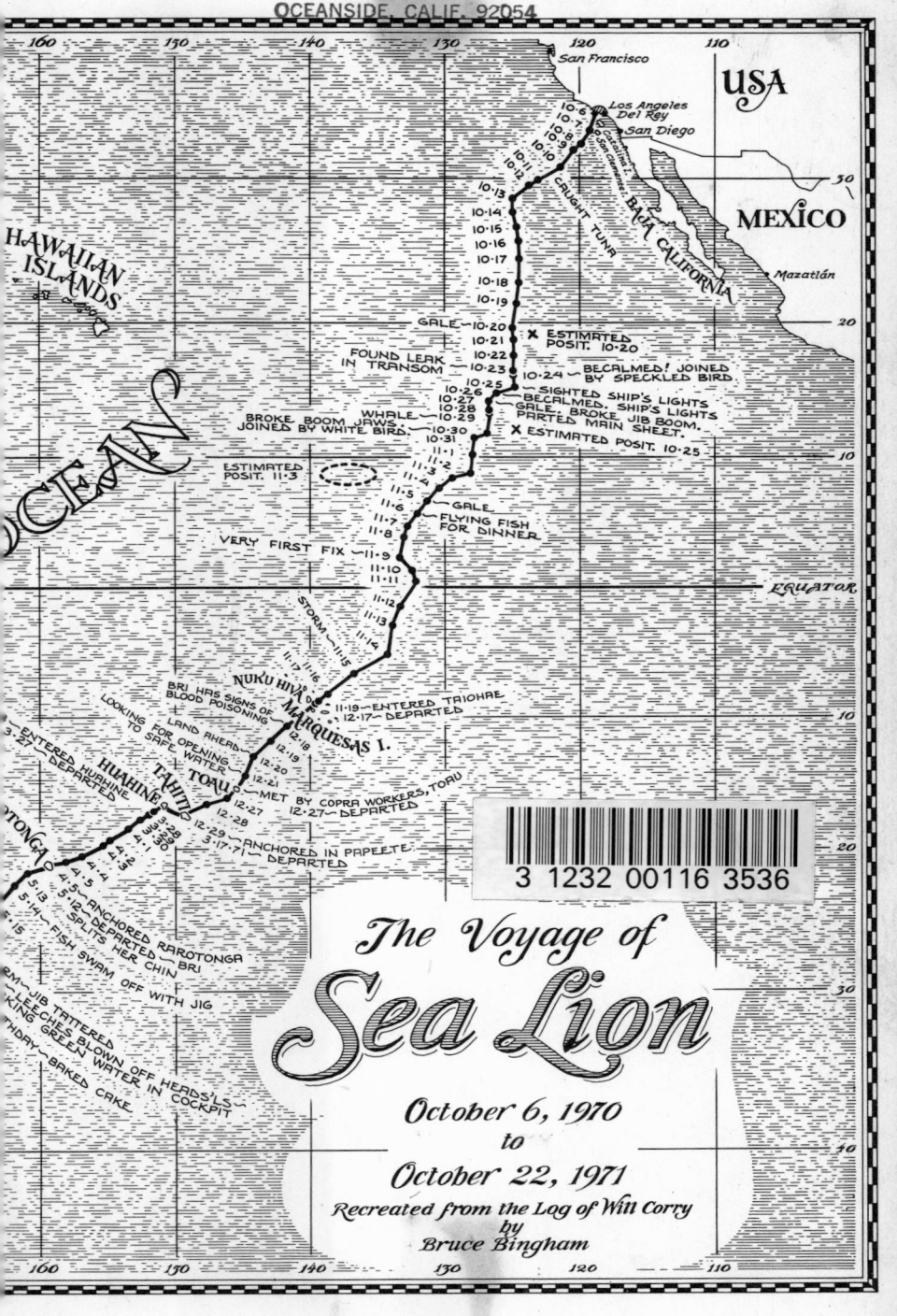

The Voyage of

Sea Lion

October 6, 1970
to
October 22, 1971

Recreated from the Log of Will Corry
by
Bruce Bingham

# THE VOYAGE OF
## Sea Lion

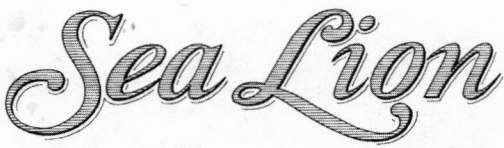

# Sea Lion

| | | | |
|---|---|---|---|
| L.O.A. | 30'6" | Draft | 4'0" |
| L.W.L. | 29'0" | Disp. | 6 tons |
| Beam | 9'0" | Sail | 500 + ♯ |

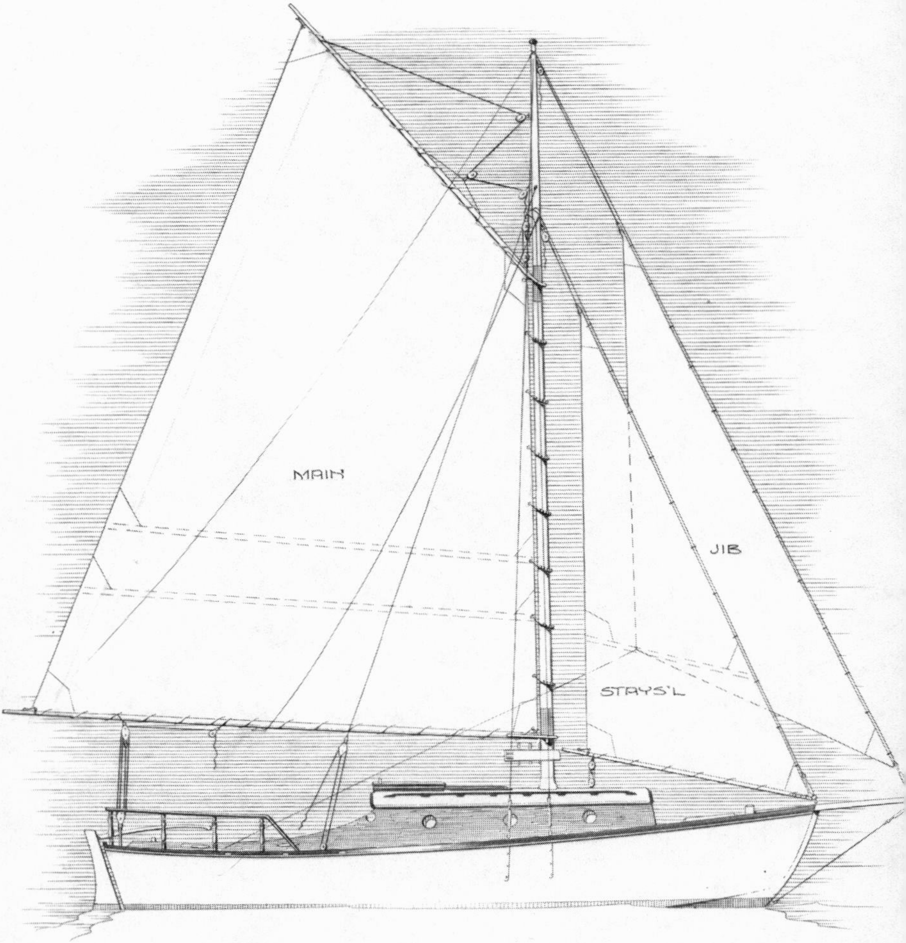

MAIN
JIB
STAYS'L
B.P. Bingham
1 3 5 7 9 11 13 15 17 19


*Rig upon departure from Del Rey, California – Oct. 6, 1970*

# THE VOYAGE OF

# Sea Lion

~~~~~~~~~~~~~~~~~~~~~~~

## by WILL CORRY

Illustrated by Bruce P. Bingham

W·W·NORTON & COMPANY·INC·NEW YORK

Library of Congress Cataloging in Publication Data

Corry, Will.
    The voyage of *Sea Lion.*

    1. Voyages and travels—1951–  2. Sea Lion (Sail-
boat)  3. Corry, Will.
G477.C83  1978    910'.41 [B]    77–14072
ISBN 0–393–03207–8

Designed by Paula Wiener
1 2 3 4 5 6 7 8 9 0

TO BRIEWFN

# Acknowledgments

I would like to thank Patrick Kirkwood, Lee Pogoler, and all who helped us prepare for this voyage.

Special thanks for the sea's permission.

# THE VOYAGE OF
*Sea Lion*

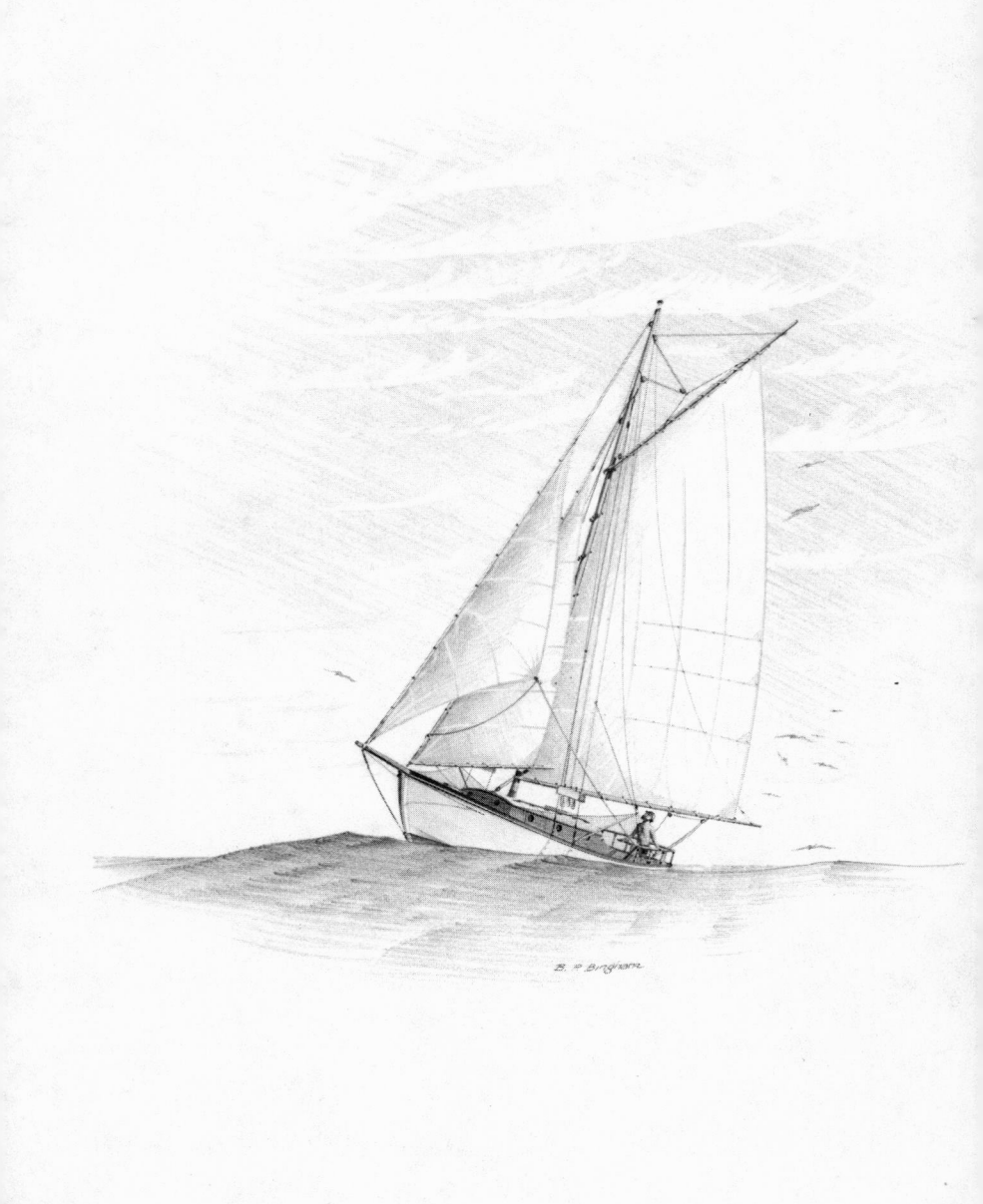

B. P. Bingham

# Chapter One

ON THE MORNING of October 6, with a cold drizzle to see us off, lines to the fuel dock were let go. My daughter was asleep below; only the puppy watched the gaff mainsail go aloft and fill lazily to a light southwest breeze.

*Sea Lion* cleared the breakwater at Marina Del Rey sooner than one would expect for a vessel so heavily laden. She headed due west. The taffrail log and spinner went over the side, and, just in case, I payed out a fishing jig on thirty feet of fifty-pound test monofilament.

*Sea Lion* was somewhere near seven years old at the time of our departure. Briewfn, my daughter, was close to three and a half. The ship's dog, Aquarius, was around ten months. I was exactly forty.

Briewfn (pronounced "Bree-A-win") and I had been together with no mama since she was eighteen months. She was listed in the logbook as "first mate." She came on deck while the California mainland was still in sight astern.

"Papa," she said, "where we going?"

"To sea," I said.

She seemed resigned but not too happy. She yawned. She was always most beautiful when first waking, with those big clear brown eyes.

We'd lived a winter in New York City writing the story that bought us this passage. We'd traveled cross-country three times horizontal and once perpendicular. We'd survived her measles in Portugal and Grandma's recom-

11

mendation for a "Christian orphan's home" in Texas. We were tight.

Briewfn was an incredibly durable person at three and a half. When she was six weeks old, she was on the road in a basket. She had flown from Los Angeles to New York when eighteen months old . . . by herself.

"Papa, I'm hungry."

The stove wasn't gimbaled.

"How about porridge?"

"Okay."

About the middle of the morning we often had porridge. As the multi-grain cereal finished cooking, honey was added. When the pot came off the fire, butter was added. A bit of milk, and we shared the pot between us with a spoon each.

Aquarius, listed as the "ship's dog," was growing more confident of the moving deck. He had quickly learned to pee only in the cockpit, which had drains. Now he shat only forward near the samson post. One more turd in the mainsheet coil might have cost him his life.

*Sea Lion* was making about three knots according to the taffrail log. By twilight Point Fermin and Los Angeles Harbor lights ranged off the port beam. How quickly those vibrations of life ashore lose their force just a few miles out!

By nightfall the wind failed but Catalina Island was astern. There was little to do but keep watch and top up the running lights with kerosene. It was quiet with the sheets drawn tight.

*Sea Lion* rolled gently to a southern swell. The "kid katchers" rose and fell in white light from the stern lantern. The two small gimbaled lamps glowed warmly down in the cabin. Briewfn was asleep in her forepeak nest. It was fashioned so she always had a lee bunk, but it *was* the forepeak and had an uncomfortable motion in a seaway. Becalmed, it was perfect. I took a time-expo-

sure picture with the camera braced against the companionway bulkhead. She was a beautiful child with long
blond hair, and her bangs were growing out.

Dawn brought a southwest breeze. Under way, the
"kid katchers" worked to perfection. The lee side was
always down and the weather side up. They were fashioned from heavy nylon cord in a four-inch mesh. Junc-
tion points were tied with waxed sail twine. The weather
jib sheet lay limp across the topping lift and helped the
wind hold the hoe-handle boom vertical. Anything that
went over the side to leeward fell into a big hammock
laced to the toe rail, and anything going over the weather
side first hit an upright net. They were not in the way.

Briewfn came on deck rubbing sleep from big brown
eyes. She was small for three and a half, Brief I sometimes called her. Most people shortened her name to
"Bri" (Bree). "Papa." A yawn. "I'm hungry." Aquarius
agreed. The wind was freshening but the seas were still
calm enough to make pancakes. The course at this stage
was as due west as conditions would allow. With wind
forward of the beam, no hand was needed at the tiller.
Pancakes were made from a mix, but the eggs were fresh,
the condensed milk whole, and the olive oil real. Molas-
ses for syrup and milk from powder to drink.

After breakfast Bri wanted "lap time." Lap time was an
established custom since the days she rode in my lap at
the steering wheel of the van. Ever since then I'd been
trying to get her to stop playing with my ear while she
sucked her thumb. Aquarius wanted "lap time" too. The
dishes needed washing, and the wind was freshening.

The swells were changing their nature to that of deep
water. Cortez Bank was in view off the port bow. The
"first mate" was growing pale and quiet. A very unusual
condition for her. Soon she vomited pancakes over the
cockpit coaming and looked back up at me with such a
questioning and pathetic gaze it was some moments be-

fore I realized her concern was for the mess she'd made on deck.

"Papa, let's go back."

I washed her face in seawater and helped her below, but she wouldn't stay. She lay quietly, bundled up on the lee cockpit bench seat looking at me as Cortez Bank slipped past on the port beam. She was never seasick again.

The mainland of California was over the horizon astern by nightfall. At least forty-eight hours without sleep. Growing excitement of having "escaped" was pure adrenaline. Yet I felt it was still too soon, still within reach of the grief and paranoia astern.

Webster says paranoia is a disease, sometimes long undetected, says the cause is really what we want to do to "them." That seems about right. The fate of those causing that grief in 1970 would have been precarious left in my hands. Their fate was not in my hands; soon, neither would mine be in theirs.

There must be a coconut tree somewhere with a stream running under it that nobody owns.

The wind failed before midnight. *Sea Lion* was becalmed with current set in her favor. Sails sheeted flat amidships ploffed and phlapped gently, checking the hull's roll. I topped up the oil in the lamps and lay down on the cockpit bench seat with a pillow under my head. Several hours passed before the vessel's change of motion woke me. Aquarius was nuzzled up asleep at my feet as though I'd never beaten hell out of him. He woke and came forward to lick my face while I lay there and tried to figure out what was happening. The sky was overcast and low. *Sea Lion* no longer rolled. A gentle wind had come up out of the west to press on the flattened sails. Simply paying out the sheets brought her to life.

At this stage of the voyage entries were going into the logbook every few waking minutes. Compass headings

were written in numbers the Navy way I'd learned. Wind velocity was almost always exaggerated in light of later experience. About this time I made the "Destination" entry: Marquesas.

During the two months' preparation for sailing my thoughts had been on the Caribbean. Now there was need for sea room. Time to learn to handle the vessel better and to learn navigation. I needed room for mistakes.

Having picked our destination, I was below going through charts to see what I had on the South Pacific. All charts were there to and through the Panama Canal and for most of the Caribbean Sea. Bri awoke. I knew that when buying the charts in San Pedro, provision for misfortune had been made. Those charts necessary in case we were set west from Panama.

"Mornin'. How d'ya feel?"

"Fine."

"Are you hungry?"

"Thirsty."

"Get yourself a drink of water and I'll fix us something in a little while."

Bri crawled down out of her "nest" forward and stumbled past me. She stopped for a hug and went to the top of the companionway ladder where she could reach the wobble pump on the stainless sink. Her tin cup hung on a hook. By the sound of her drinking I knew she was looking at me.

There were just four applicable charts on board. One for all the Marquesas, one for Nuku Hiva Harbor. One for the Tuamotu Archipelago, and one for the entire central South Pacific.

Porridge for breakfast, and we continued as west as possible into the westerlies the rest of that day.

It was becoming evident that the "mate" and the "ship's dog" were not very fond of each other. They

were in competition for my attention. Attention that was growing more scarce as the experience unfolded. Any show of affection for one brought the other in a jealous fit. Bri was insistent. She'd bring a string and one of her stuffed animals to have it tied around the neck. Then she'd look at Aquarius and go get another string. I'd refuse to tie it around the willing animal's neck and she'd complain bitterly.

Fortunately Bri's favorite evening meal was spaghetti. There was a great quantity on board. The sauce was made by first sautéing a couple of diced onions in olive oil, adding a dry mix doctored with tomato paste and real garlic. Even the ship's dog liked it.

Sundown found Venus in the starboard shrouds and a full moon on the port bow. The wind didn't die that night. We sailed on with a free helm and wind forward of the starboard beam.

It was my custom to go over the cabin top fore and aft when in a hurry. Jumping down into the darkened cockpit, half the time I landed square in the middle of the ship's dog. The poor animal became so frightened to see me coming, day or night, he'd freeze. Right in my path! He seemed always underfoot or tangled in the sheets trying to flee.

Around midnight it rained and Aquarius came into the cabin through the lee portlight. One would think he was a dachshund instead of an Australian sheep dog. He never used the ladder. There had been a few land birds, but I hadn't seen another vessel the previous day. Fatigue was beginning to add up. It numbed the brain and put hands and feet out of sync. I welcomed a nap before morning.

Some routines were emerging into a daily pattern. First on waking, put the pot on and grind the coffee beans. Then forward to scrub down after the ship's dog with a wire brush while the water came to a boil. While

Briewfn still slept, I could have my toilet sitting on the lee rail with a cup of coffee in hand and watch the sunrise. It was joyous. Once she awoke, my attention to duty was divided. "Papa, how about pancakes today?" Pancakes were my least favorite meal; it meant plates to wash.

At this point I would not have considered moving through the water without trolling a fish jig. Experience had already taught me to stow the fine new Penn Senator reel with its fifty-pound test Dacron line. There was nothing sporting about it. I was after meat. The jig was now tied off solid to a cleat by hundred-pound test monofilament. I was looking straight at the fishline when suddenly it twanged taut. Trying not to get excited, I brought the fish in hand over hand, letting the line fall at my feet. It broke the surface a ten-pound tuna! When it landed in the cockpit, Aquarius freaked out and Bri laughed and danced while I became tangled in thirty feet of monofilament. That fish flippity-flopped all over the cockpit area, scattering breakfast dishes and tying the line in knots, while I tried desperately to dodge the double-hook jig.

It was afternoon before that mess was squared away. I cut the small tuna into steaks and ruined it by using too much seasoning. Aquarius wouldn't even eat it.

That night the wind shifted to northerly. I took it as an omen. Away west we romped on a broad reach.

By morning there was no sign of birds anywhere. We tore along west for nearly three more days, with sleep every night. *Sea Lion* had a comfortable, tractor-like motion. Nine foot of beam on a twenty-five-foot waterline. The cockpit was enormous, with turned dowel mahogany taffrail. She was cutter-rigged with yankee jib and boomed staysail. She was my first sailboat. Just a little over two months before, we had "liberated" her from Southern California character boat status.

Dead reckoning said we were at the 125th meridian. Fourteen days out of L.A. and the log read 553 nautical miles. With that same northerly wind we payed out the sheets and headed south.

# Chapter Two

THAT WAS OUR COURSE for the next three thousand miles. One-eighty, due south.

We were free at last! We had "escaped," my daughter, the ship's dog, and I! We were away in the open sea! With the wind first on one quarter and then the other, *Sea Lion* had escaped too.

The only book I had read on the subject of cruising in a sailboat was *Sailing Alone Around the World,* by Joshua Slocum. There was no doubt I had our necks stuck way out. It kept me hopping! Bri had plenty of opportunity to watch examples of a daily preached lesson: "One hand for your work, one hand for the vessel." That child was incredible. She never had to be told when the weather was too rough for her to be on the cabin top. As the wind would pick up, she'd use both hands and climb down into the cockpit. If it increased, she went below, but resisted the lee bunk till the last moment. She was rapidly becoming very strong. The constant motion of a sailing vessel is a total body builder. Muscles that shore life let atrophy live. We weren't ten days out before her favorite sport was swinging out over the cockpit from the weather running backstay.

There were moments I could spend with her, but mostly she had to look out for herself. She didn't like that at all and kept the pressure on for attention. So did Aquarius.

Despite her advanced years, Bri was still taking an

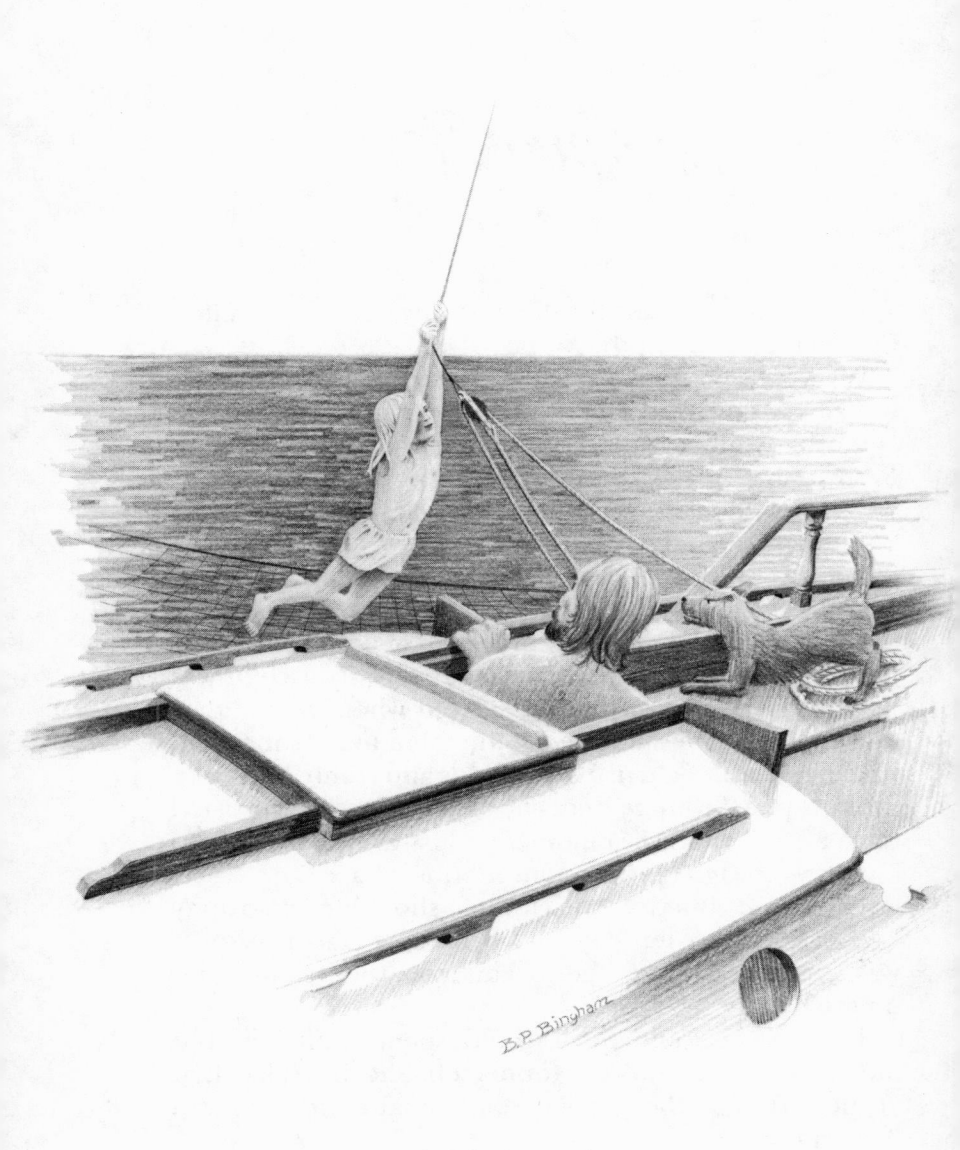

B.P.Bingham

afternoon nap. She was starting to rebel. "Papa, dammit, I don't want to go to sleep!" She'd be sitting heavy-eyed on the edge of the lee bunk playing with her stuffed critters.

"If you don't rest, you can't look out for yourself and *Sea Lion* will bust you." Then I'd scramble on deck to try and save a jibe. In a few minutes I'd hear her head thud the mast. She'd curse it and go to sleep. For two blessed hours! Those were my hours. It was the only time there was to study books, or do anything else the sea would allow.

I didn't know a lot about jibes and maybe you don't. A jibe is when the wind spills forward around in back of the mainsail. Suddenly the broad-off boom swaps sides. It is spooky because the sail is out of sync with the hull. It *can* happen before the wind even reaches dead astern. Depends on what the sea wants to let you get away with.

*Sea Lion* had been bettering a hundred miles a day. Not bad for a twenty-nine-foot boat. Her only self-steering was a method of lashing the tiller. An endless quarter-inch nylon line ran from the tiller's end through pad eyes on the cockpit coaming. There were jam cleats handy on both sides of the coaming. With the wind aft and both headsails sheeted flat, the tiller could be held to weather and quickly released if she went for jibe.

Soon the northerlies eased up. During one of Bri's afternoon naps I decided to break out the giant new jib. I had ordered it made in Wilmington. Its purpose was to make *Sea Lion* more like Slocum's *Spray*. It replaced both the headsails. The forestay was struck and lashed out of the way to the shrouds. The giant jib was hoisted on the jibstay and its clubfoot sheeted to the staysail traveler on the cabin top. The sheet was two-blocked down tight to the traveler, holding that giant triangle of sail flat amidships.

It acted as a vane and kept *Sea Lion*'s nose downwind.

Much less weather helm was needed, and it cut the accidental jibes down to about one a day. I could lash the tiller and sleep every night the sea permitted, and I was learning to sleep with one eye when it didn't.

By now the weather was warming up. *Sea Lion* was gaining on the southbound sun.

It was a relief to be in cut-offs and barefoot, but it took some time for bruised toes to discover where the deck fittings were. Bri and I could find moments to sit on the foredeck, lean back against the cabin, and read *Scuppers, the Sailor Dog.*

If there is anything I hate doing, it's washing dishes. Especially more than once in a row. It's so damned mundane while your head is flying around in celestial navigation. Soon there would be a dishpan full of the damned things sliding and banging around in the cockpit. The "mate" wasn't the only one who had to learn things the hard way. From the day I got a fork in the foot, those dishes were always washed and put away before I even rolled a smoke.

I was just getting used to the comforts of that giant jib when the wind pulled around from south. The giant would draw fine until *Sea Lion* was about fifty degrees to the wind, though it did bury the bow some. Try as I might, she would not come into the wind. That meant that if anything fell into the sea I could not go back to retrieve it. The giant jib was struck and stowed in its sail bag.

With the two headsails back up, she was handy to come about. She was her old self, you might say, and when the wind was aft, the jibes increased. When below, I could feel the goosey wallow, and on deck the headsails blew out from behind the mainsail just before the boom smashed across with a terrible force. I could stand anywhere in the cockpit and the boom cleared my head; it was the mainsheet fall that often caught me just

reaching the tiller release. I could save ten violent jibes in a row and the eleventh would threaten to tear the mast out.

I had not yet made that first attempt to shoot and work out a celestial fix. Dead reckoning said we were due west of the Gulf of Tehuantepec; on (or near) the 125th meridian. It was clouding up. The wind pulled around out of northeast and freshened. That put it on the quarter and we flew away on course. The wind was blowing hard but the seas weren't high . . . yet. Everybody got excited. Bri and Aquarius actually played together! I started baking bread in the Dutch oven. The wind and seas could be seen from the companionway ladder. So long as the mate and ship's dog were clear of that path to the tiller, we flew. From my perch I could actually see the hands move on the log's dial.

The Dutch oven was a dumb thing with Pyrex doors that covered both burners of the kerosene Primus stove. That oven was built for a house trailer. On such a small vessel there was little space to stow it . . . even when it did cool. Before the oven was put away, the wind pulled north and increased. More often came mad dashes, with daughter, ship's dog, and dolls sent flying, in a race for the tiller.

Bri took a chunk of the fresh bread, a piece of cheese, and the last apple. She looked at the weather and headed for the lee bunk. I should have known it was going to blow then. The seas were high and cross from the wind shift. I had supper of fresh bread at the tiller. No longer could the tiller be lashed. The angle between terrific weather helm and jibe narrowed. On she flew!

I had never reefed the main. By now it was too late. The seas were much too high and darkness was coming on. By nightfall the wind was increasing and the narrowing angle steerable was then between jibe and broaching to in those monstrous seas. The sound of wind and sea

became a moan. That full mainsail started burying the hull, and the bow wave grew enormous.

All that could be done was keep her stern to the wind, not let her jibe, and yet keep her nose downwind. I dared not let the wind get anywhere near the quarter, for I knew that, in spite of her large rudder and long tiller, there was not the strength to keep her from going into the trough. Likewise, a jibe in that wind could easily dismast her. The angle narrowed. I sat there with about three degrees in which the tiller just felt mushy, one more degree in either direction and we were in deep trouble. If I could only leave the tiller long enough to throw off the peak halyard and scandalize the main, that would help. I had to try it. The flashlight beam showed that the coil had already been washed off the belaying pin, but the hitch held fast. Letting the tiller ease started to bring her bow up. I held it just where there was plenty of strain, nudged it a bit more, jammed the tiller rope in the jam cleat. A mad dash in darkness to the starboard shrouds to throw the halyard off and, when the headsails blew out behind my butt, twice as fast back to the tiller to save the jibe. It worked. The mainsail was scandalized. The strain eased. The angle widened some, and on we roared. All night.

*Sea Lion* was moving fast but not surfing. All that sail had her buried. Occasionally she'd bust a cross wave full on the beam. It was a collision at an intersection! *Sea Lion* would shudder, shake it off, and roar along into the night. Just before daylight the wind increased and took away the advantage of scandalized main. The angle narrowed again to about three degrees.

Had I not been so busy and could I have seen those seas through the night, surely I would have been terrified. Daylight came and it was terrifying. What could it be? A Mexican storm this far out? Hell, we were a thousand miles from Mexico!

By good light a wailing sound was added to the sea's

moan. The sails had to come down. Broach or no, I had to let her come up into the wind. She surprised me. She came up into those monstrous waves like a duck. The minute her sails spilled the wind, I raced forward and threw off all the halyards. Everything came down with a crash, and halyards blew in the wind.

Bri woke and came on deck. I forced her below, secured the forehatch, and dogged the portlights.

Because of the conclusions in *Heavy Weather Sailing,* I had a three-hundred-foot coil of five-eighths line ready to "drag warps." With the bitter end in hand, I scrambled back on deck. The end was secured and line payed out astern. We definitely slowed.

Snapping the safety harness onto the lifeline, I went forward. At every move the harness impeded progress. I could not work. Once it even had me around the neck! I took it off and threw it in the cockpit. When the sails were finally at least lashed down and the halyards caught up, I went below, closed and dogged the companionway hatch, and sat down on the cabin sole in total exhaustion.

"Papa, what happened?"

"The wind blew."

I could hear a lot of water sloshing in the bilge just under my butt. It was hot, stuffy, and damp down there in the cabin. Suddenly a lot of seawater crashed down on *Sea Lion!* When I slid the companionway hatch open, dead air pulsated as the cabin was turned into a wind whistle. From the deck it was obvious that we were dead in the water. Waves were breaking on us from astern. We had to get moving.

The new storm jib and storm trysail came out of their bags and, without the hindrance of harness and lifeline, I hoisted them in short order. I took in the warps. *Sea Lion* moved off before the seas, but she rolled badly. That rolling prevented cooking anything but coffee on the ungimbaled stove.

The cabin was a gooey mess of spilled flour, coffee

beans, and kerosene. Everything that could come adrift had. Bilge water was beginning to slosh from under the cabin sole. I straightened up the cabin as much as the rolling would allow, drank a cup of strong coffee laced with honey, and charged back on deck.

It was a bigger mess on deck. Fishline was tangled with the log and had a fish on it. Why do they always bite when it blows? I left it and tucked my first reef in the main. In fact, the first three. A full-reefed main was hoisted and the tiny storm jib was replaced by the yankee. *Sea Lion* ceased to roll so badly and began to sail. We rode out the rest of the day in reasonable comfort as the winds fell to about forty knots. What a mess there was to clean!

The bilge was afloat with all manner of things. I had to take the pump out of its bracket because it was so hard to clean and clogged often. With the engine cover open and pick-up hose down into the bilge, I pumped for hours into the cockpit, where it ran out the drains. When all the water was out from under the engine (the lowest point), I could still hear sloshing forward. All the cabin sole boards had to come up. The drain holes through the ribs had to be unplugged. Some of the bays hadn't been drained in so long the water was beginning to stink. The weep holes were tiny. A swollen pinto bean became a stopper! In the end I had to dry each bay with a sponge. Everything fitted *too* well on *Sea Lion*. She'd been built by M. Marnatola, a cabinetmaker from San Diego, I'm told. A cabinetmaker is not necessarily a boatbuilder. The engine cover was flush with piano hinges, also the cockpit seat lids. The piano hinges leaked, corroded, froze. Hurried raising in search of a rusted tool sent out a shower of tiny bronze wood screws, and there was the lid in hand! I cursed a lot.

# Chapter Three

BY THE TIME our first storm had blown itself out, the mate and ship's dog were bored to the point of mutiny. Her favorite book, *Scuppers,* had got wet and come apart. Aquarius's dry food was beginning to mildew. We dried her book and put it back together with tape. Sometimes a bit of beef broth mixed with the mildewed dry food would please the ship's dog. I was cleaning and oiling the taffrail log when she demanded that I read to her. She said, "Damn the log!" Not only was she starting to curse; she used the words accurately. It was a bit shocking coming from a body less than four years old.

Next day wind came out of the northwest just right. I shook reefs out of the main while Bri held the tiller, though it was obvious she'd rather suck her thumb. The wind held for another day and I got some sleep. If only sleep could have been put aboard like the stores!

Next morning the logbook entry was for October 23. Eighteen days out and still I hadn't been able to take a sight and work out our position. Every moment available had been spent on the books. I figured I had it down, but all the conditions necessary had never come together. Well, you can only see stars and the horizon at the same time for about twenty minutes at morning and again at night . . . if the sky is clear. At morning and night the mate and ship's dog were either waking up and needing food or needing it before going to sleep. The stars were not possible. I'd have to settle for the sun alone if I was ever to get a celestial fix of our position.

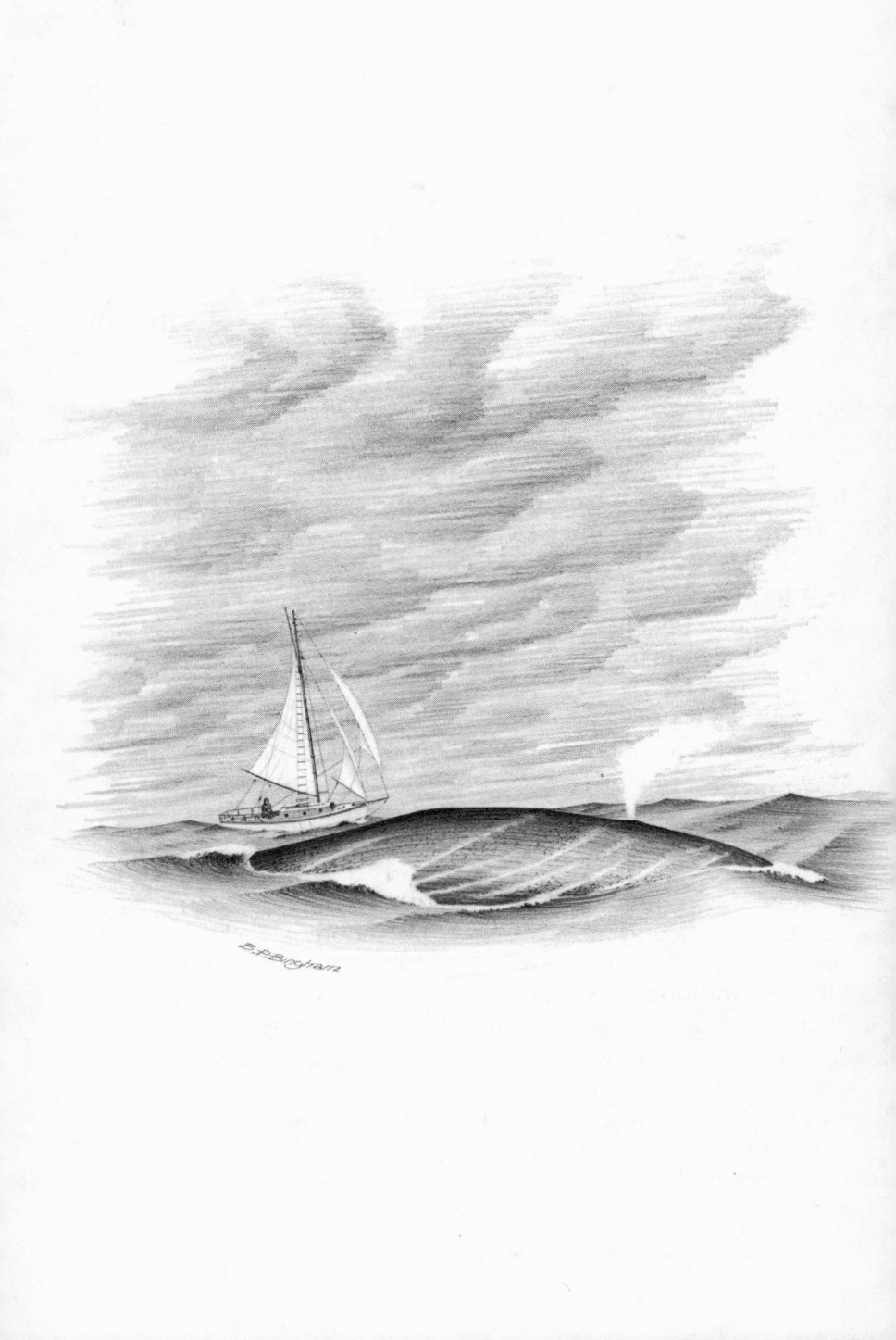

The portable transoceanic radio always got the time tics, and I used it for that purpose only. It ran on six flashlight batteries.

Near noon we were ghosting along and the horizon was flat. I broke out the plastic sextant and the stopwatch and took a "noon latitude sight." Lack of experience left me with little confidence, but I figured we were about twelve or thirteen degrees north of the equator.

The wind failed completely by midafternoon, and I started the engine just to charge the batteries. The noise and stink of it were awful. We ran on engine about three miles and I shut it off. That night was spent becalmed.

Sunrise was spectacular, setting distant thunderheads afire! I no longer reached for the camera. Trying to photograph a thing kept me from seeing it. A large speckled bird joined us and flew and flew about the masthead in quiet air. I was listening to see if I could hear its wings when I heard water sloshing in the bilge. It had recently been sponged dry and no rain or seas had come aboard.

Ten gallons were hand-pumped into the cockpit and the whole bilge sponged dry. I was afraid that the great strain on the mast might have sprung a leak in the garboards next to the keel.

The garboards were dry. Seawater was coming from the transom, where the strain of rudder had opened seams. It was discomforting. Nothing to do but pump it daily.

That night we were becalmed again. Just after dark there were lights of a passing ship up ahead. If that vessel was en route from Panama to Hawaii, it tended to confirm our dead reckoning position. Before daylight there was another on the same course.

Morning brought squalls, and mare's tails were fanned out from the north over our position. All day we dodged through sudden squalls, tucking reefs in and shaking

them out. By nightfall we were becalmed, with the lights of another ship passing in the distance, this time astern. No sleep. The feeling was that of being stalled in the middle of a freeway. I'd been aboard enough ships as a watch-standing seaman to know that a lookout for such as *Sea Lion* was a joke. The captain wouldn't even spill his coffee on impact. We needed wind.

Just before dawn a *gale* of wind came out of the north. The main was reefed in darkness, and I struck the yankee jib. Hardly had we settled on our course before the wind did a one-eighty and became a gale out of the south! The seas had gone mad! Figuring we were something east of the 125th meridian, I put her on a port tack to west. I could not get *Sea Lion* to heave to. Inexperience is one thing; combined with brain-scrambling fatigue, the attempt was disheartening. Every time I'd try the maneuver, she'd either come on about or "go into irons."

Suddenly there was a loud *crack!* The staysail boom had parted! Then the sheet strap on the main boom carried away.

In order to get a line on the boom, it was necessary to take her downwind with the main broad off and shrouds acting as the only sheet. When she got some speed up, I shoved the tiller hard over as though to come about. That brought the boom swinging in close enough to lasso. The staysail was struck, and *Sea Lion* beat on with a single line for a mainsheet.

The mate and ship's dog were in a world all their own. Regardless of what was happening on the other side of the gunwale, they stayed glued to their purpose of gaining total attention. It was maddening! But at least I didn't have to explain or justify my mistakes to the likes of those two. I too was in a world all my own. By late afternoon the wind shifted to the east, and by nightfall we were becalmed in high cross seas. It was most uncomfortable and stayed that way. Around midnight fatigue took its toll and I slept till near dawn.

The seas had flattened out some when frenzied barking woke me. On deck the sky was overcast and there was little light. Bri woke and came up the ladder. I could see nothing in the direction Aquarius was freaking . . . then we heard it breathe!

The ship's dog knew it was no fish. It was a whale! At last something beyond the gunwale caught their attention. By good light it was apparent that the whale was more than twice as long as *Sea Lion.* The wind: light, fitful, and southerly. That critter stayed with us all day while I replaced the mainsheet strap and fashioned a scarf in the staysail boom. It seemed perfectly content with the vessel's slow pace, surfacing first on one side, then on the other. Aquarius was going nuts trying to guess where it would surface next in order to breathe. The critter stayed submerged too long at a time to keep Bri's attention.

"Papa, read *Sailor Dog* to me."

"No. Go away."

"Then how about lap time?"

"Briewfn. Can't you see I'm trying to get this rain catcher finished?"

"It's not raining."

Not only were we beginning to run low on water, Aquarius had started peeing up on the step in the cockpit where the engine cover was. The water-tank filler cap was there too. The thought of having our water supply contaminated with dog piss was enough to send me into a rage. No matter how many times I beat him, he seemed locked to that spot. In fact, all that was necessary was for me to raise my voice in anger. He'd pee on the water-tank cap and flee forward. He was very agile, and I could not catch him on deck.

The whale stayed about twenty-five yards off either side and was definitely friendly. I felt a kinship to the beast and wondered what it must think of all the commotion on the little sailboat.

We ghosted through the night, but there was little sleep. The ship's dog set up a frenzied clamor each time the whale took a breath out in the darkness. When I hollered and threw a sneaker at him, he peed on the water tank and fled. It was better to let him bark.

Come daylight, that whale was still alongside. The wind came light out of the east and it started to rain.

The rain catcher was a trough under the main boom made of rubberized nylon cloth. Short stick spreaders held it open and to the boom. A hose was attached near the gooseneck and ran down to the filler cap in the cockpit. Just as it was finished, the rain stopped. The wind freshened and pulled around east-northeast.

*Sea Lion* romped along and the whale kept up while I pumped the bilge again. *Sea Lion* was beginning to look very ragged. Varnish was peeling in great layers off the cabin sides, loose ends of rubbery deck caulking fluttered all along the deck seams.

Although she looked like hell, *Sea Lion* was once again under full sails and romping south. In the afternoon that whale decided on a westerly course and we parted company. I baked a batch of sea biscuits. Those biscuits were proving a staple. This batch was so good I entered the recipe in the logbook.

We were all in exceptionally good health. Of course Bri was thriving; she had nothing to do but eat, sleep, play with her dolls, fight the ship's dog, and avoid my rages.

The only mirror on board was on the bulkhead in front of the toilet. I never used the toilet; that was Bri's domain. She'd stand on the closed lid for hours watching herself perform in the reflection. This night I brought the stern lantern in to have a look at my whiskers.

They were almost a beard now, the first one I'd ever grown. The face was very brown in lantern light, hair tangled and sun-bleached. The eyes were crazy-looking.

Suddenly I felt something wet slosh at my feet. It proved to be toilet water!

With the wind on the starboard quarter, the toilet was on the lee side and shipping water! Bri was never very good about flushing it. It was a stinking and dangerous mess. I closed the through-hull valves, but still the water came in. It's one thing to have foul weather cut into sleep; a fouled toilet is quite another. I gently jibed to the other quarter so the toilet no longer shipped water, and went to sleep on the lee cockpit seat.

Daylight came and the mess still faced me. With visions of hepatitis racing through the crew, I set to work. The whole thing had to be practically dismantled. All manner of kid's toy parts were jammed in the mechanism. A plastic bubble-making toy was stuck in the exhaust valve. After it was cleaned up and the whole area washed down with disinfectant, I made breakfast.

After porridge, the wind pulled northeast and began to howl. A reef went in the main, and it started to rain. It rained hard. By noon there were twelve gallons of new water in the tank. I had stood constant guard against contamination.

Dead reckoning was getting to be anybody's guess. I'd been keeping track by drawing lines of course and distance on those little plotting sheets where you write in the longitude and latitude. There was a handful of them. The Pilot chart, that blessing of the ages, said I should put a bit west to make up for the set of current. I did so and accidentally jibed. It was the last tolerable jibe. The main boom gooseneck parted!

Although it was made of heavy bronze casting, the gooseneck actually exploded, causing an L-shaped tear in the main. It was dark by the time the mainsail was on deck and unlaced from boom and gaff. All the while, it rained like hell. Once again the giant jib came out of its sail bag. I sent it aloft hanked to the port shrouds for a

mainsail. At least it dampened the roll. Spaghetti for supper.

I lay down and tried to figure out just how boom jaws were to be fashioned from the materials on board. Sleep crept up.

Hard rain had ceased by morning, but the sky was gray. Two white birds were circling close around the vessel. No time to watch white birds. Not even a second cup of coffee. The pieces were selected from an assortment of hardwood scraps. The boom jaws were to be made from oak and ash one-bys. Sandwiched cross grain and through-bolted with quarter-inch bronze carriage bolts. It seemed simple, but interruptions by mate, meals, and ship's dog, aided by the vessel's awkward and unpredictable motion, caused evening to catch us with little done. Those white birds had increased to three, and the boom jaws weren't even half finished.

The wind shifted to south, with interrupted rain and unruly seas. *Sea Lion* just slogged and jounced west in the fitful weather all that night.

The first gray light of morning revealed seven white birds roosting on the taffrail. They were tuckered out and made no effort to leave while I ground coffee beans at the companionway ladder. So still were they Aquarius hadn't even seen them. They appeared to be egrets. I assumed they were land birds since their feet were not webbed. We were a thousand miles from any land. When I came on deck with coffee in hand and headed for the lee rail, four of the birds became airborne. Aquarius freaked. The remaining three just sat there and glared at him. The barking woke Bri. She was delighted with the company. They were pure white with yellow beaks and legs. They moved to the farthest point on the taffrail away from me and glared.

When work started on the boom jaws, two of the birds flew. Six were in the air and one remained glaring from

the taffrail. Their flight was a tireless thing, as though
they were powered by wound-up rubber bands that re-
wound with each wing stroke. I fancied I could hear tiny
pin hinges squeak!

All day, while I was sawing, drilling, rasping, fitting,
and refitting the jaw pieces to the boom, those six white
birds flew and flew around the mast. At nightfall, as we
withdrew to the cabin, four of them lit on the taffrail to
join the one who'd stayed there all day. The two in the
air flew away in ever-widening circles. Falling asleep, I
imagined they had been blown to sea by a storm, possibly
from some swamp on the South American coast.

Next morning Bri woke before my coffee, so great was
her interest in the birds. Only one was there. To us it
seemed to be a female. We named her Capella. She kept
a glaring eye on the day's work. Aquarius got too close
and received a sharp peck on the nose. After that Capella
was more sure of herself and hopped down into the
cockpit. Bri got her some water, but she wouldn't drink.
At midday lunch break we offered a can of sardines. She
wouldn't touch it and glared at us as though we'd in-
sulted her.

The wind was a good Force 5 and kept *Sea Lion* reaching soggily west with a free helm. By nightfall the boom
jaw "sandwich" was ready to assemble and secure to the
boom, but supper had to be fixed.

That night Capella came into the galley and slept on
the stove.

Next morning she walked back and forth glaring while
I ground the coffee beans. She wasn't getting in the way
of my coffee! I picked her up. She was weightless. She
glared me in the eye and pecked weakly. I tossed her out
into the cockpit and lit the stove.

It was necessary to take the end of the boom down into
the cabin to fit the boom jaws because the south wind was
driving sheets of rain.

Aquarius was getting braver and delighted in crowding Capella all over the vessel. Presently she'd had enough and came back into the cabin. The stove was still too warm, so she hopped down on the weather bunk and glared at us defiantly. Still she would not eat anything we had to offer, nor would she drink water. How she had anything to dump I'll never know, but she did. Right on the bunk! Once again she found herself in the cockpit.

With Bri's help she managed to stay one hop ahead of the ship's dog. Bri wanted desperately to pick the bird up and pet her. Capella's reaction to any approach was awesome. She'd rear back on her tail feathers, spread both wings, ruffle her neck feathers, open her beak, glare, and sort of hiss. The rain wasn't cold and had lightened some, so I continued to work and let the three of them have at it.

It was hell to get the mate down for a nap that day. She insisted Capella needed her and even called me a "big shit." Bri was just asleep and I was lacing the mainsail to the boom when I heard Capella squawk for the first time. In her flight to escape Aquarius, she'd fallen over the side into the "kid katcher" off the port bow. One wing was completely tangled in nylon cord. She thrashed and squawked weakly. I had to cut several of the cords to free her. Capella was, except for a cushion or two, the only thing the katchers had caught. Her squawks woke Bri. She was really angry and took it out on Aquarius.

This was the fourth day since the gooseneck parted. Still the press was against us out of the south. As long as the mainsail was that jib hanked to the shrouds, all we could do was run back and forth across the south wind. According to the Pilot chart, the current was setting us easterly twenty-five miles a day.

Finally the mainsail was ready to be hoisted. Once it was up, I had expected we would beat into that south wind with great authority. Not so. *Sea Lion* was no wind-

ward racer! I reefed the main and just let her luff along southwest for comfort and pumped the bilge again. The bilge water was turning sweet. The deck leaked like a sieve.

While we ate supper of red beans and corn bread (smothered in catsup for Bri), Aquarius ignored his mildewed food and went after Capella. We heard the squawk and scuffle. They were on the foredeck. Aquarius had her held down with his paws and her feathers were all wet where he had been mouthing her. There was no blood and Bri said, "Look, he's kissing her!" He was, too. Just slobbering, mouthing, and licking her, pleased as hell her pecking was too weak to have effect. We freed her, and Bri, delighted at her weakness too, took her below.

Bri had long since refused her bunk in the forepeak, and I'd rigged the weather bunk for her. Aquarius slept on the cabin sole, Capella on the stove. The lee bunk was mine . . . when I had a chance to get in it.

I didn't sleep well and had downed my second cup of coffee long before daylight. Rain had stopped and the wind died down. Capella was very weak. Her eyelids stayed half closed even as she glared in defiance. The rubber bands were broken. Light from the stern lantern just balanced coming dawn as I handed her over the lee rail to the sea. She made no protest as the white dot receded in the wake.

As though a spell were broken, the wind came out of the southwest fresh. We trimmed sails and came about to take it on the starboard beam. *Sea Lion* came to life.

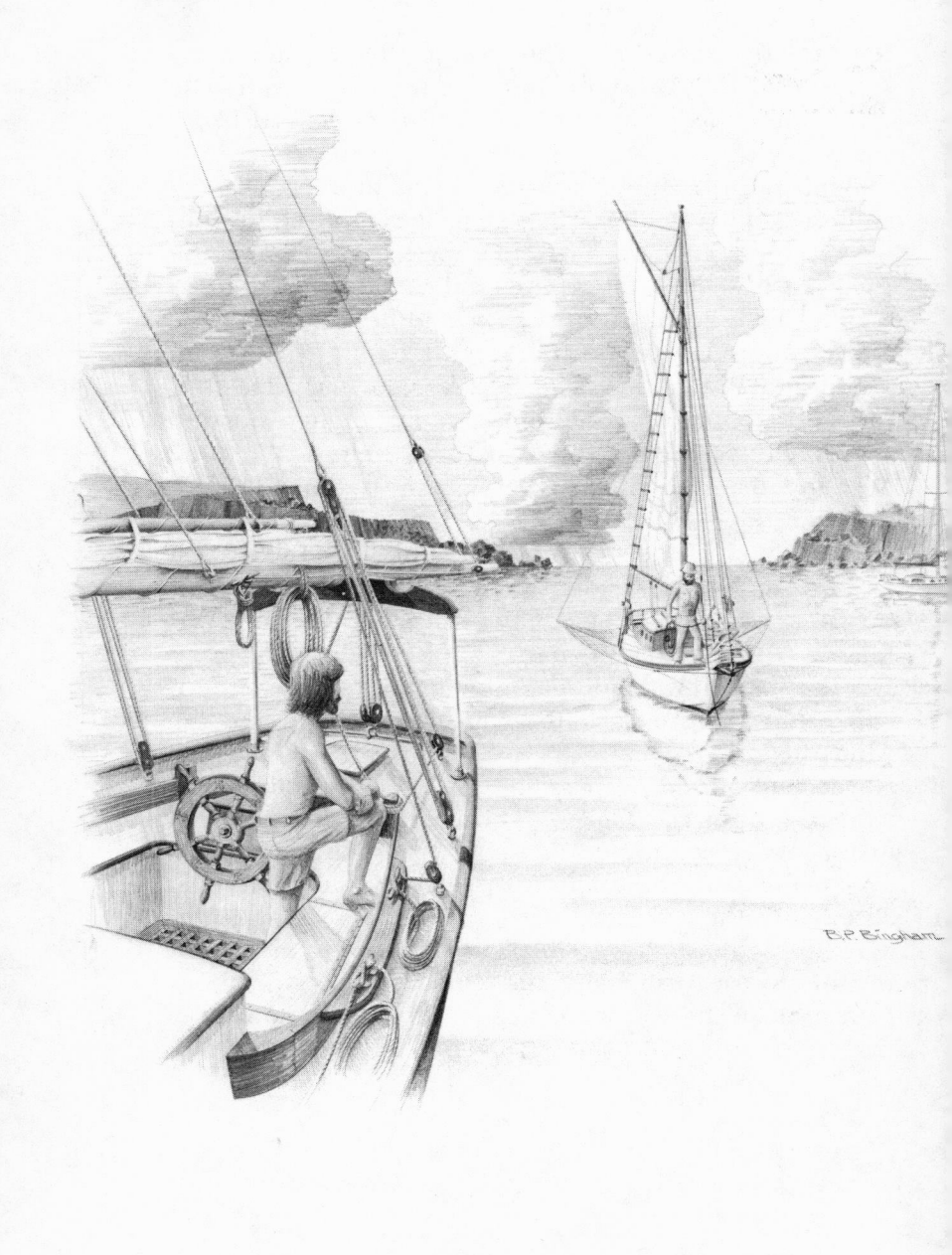

B.P. Bingham

# Chapter Four

THE SEXTANT BEGAN to fit my hand. Somehow it just knew when a sight was right on. Reminded me of childhood times with a .22; before the bullet left the barrel I knew. Even when the seas were high and the horizon just bumps, that sun image would set right halfway between the bumps. Click! After that it was just numbers. Add or subtract. Look it up in the right tables in the proper book. Mark it on the chart. I still didn't know if it worked. There was a feeling it did, but I still didn't *know*. It had better. My dead reckoning by now was impossible to follow. We were thirty days out.

Bri didn't carry on about Capella the way I thought she would. Out of sight out of mind. For days now we had been on a port tack with the wind generally out of the southeast. The weather was really warm. Sun was bright daily, sometimes with puffy white high-pressure clouds. *Sea Lion* was sawing the miles off comfortably, lying about forty-five degrees to the wind. No hand was needed at the tiller and no jibes! Instead of calms, we had found the southeast trades north of the equator.

Life was beginning to appear on the starboard top-sides. It had been creeping up above the waterline for days. We stayed on the port tack because of the easterly current set, thirty miles a day now.

Sometimes Bri and I would lie in the lee kid katcher, one leg hooked around a shroud just in case. I'd hold her. For hours we'd lie there with the sea sizzling by

inches under us. Looking up at the sails working and basking in that delicious sunshine!

Once while I was washing the supper dishes at sundown, a flying fish landed in my lap. We had him for dessert. The closer we got to the equator the more the wind pulled east. It was joyous! Day followed nights without a cloud in the sky. We could see every star from horizon to horizon.

On November 9 the first "fix" was entered in the log: 2°12'N x 133°36'W. That day also found the southeast wind failing. On the morning of the tenth, after calms, the wind came due out of the east. Force 5. It was the best of all possible worlds! A broad reach! I'd take a sun sight in the morning and cross it with a noon latitude sight. 1°10'N x 132°39'W at noon on the tenth.

*Sea Lion* crossed the equator before noon on November 11. Noon entry: 00°30'S x 132°16'W.

On the morning of the thirteenth there was a strange occurrence. The sun was just above the eastern horizon and the full moon the same distance above the western. The sky was absolutely cloudless. *Sea Lion* was smack between full moon and sun! Unknown forces had the seas pulled all out of shape . . . and affected my head likewise. Bri and Aquarius felt it too. Suddenly porpoises were leaping everywhere around us! It was a magical, mystical time. We could not speak.

Those living things on the starboard topsides were beginning to develop personalities. They were rubbery critters with beaked mouths and hair for tongues. Some of them were the size of my thumb. Small ones were even growing on the spinning taffrail log. I'd strip them off with my thumbnail and put them in a pot with spinach noodles and cook them. The dish was delicious. Starboard remained the lee side and they continued to grow. *Sea Lion* was slowing down even though the wind freshened.

Just a little over five degrees below the equator I brought the wind on the quarter and started a "closing action" on the Marquesas Islands . . . if, indeed, they were there. I expected the jibes to return with the wind aft. They didn't. The tiller in a notch ever so slightly to weather, headsails flat, and the main broad off, she would run all day and never offer to jibe! It was the seas. They were absolutely constant. In that part of the world they had always been the same. *Scuppers, the Sailor Dog* could be read twice a day! Aquarius shat in great comfort forward, and there was sleep every night.

We were forty days out of Los Angeles when the entry for "Estimated Time of Arrival" went in the logbook. In three days *Sea Lion* would once more be in shoal water . . . if those islands were actually there.

Once the entry was made, I did not sleep well. I figured the horizon was about seven miles from *Sea Lion*'s deck. She could easily cover fifty while I slept. In fact, she made such good time that first night after the entry of ETA I had to move it up a half day. With land expected on the morrow, there was no sleep . . . till dawn. I climbed the shrouds at the first crack of light and saw nothing. Numb and disheartened, I lay down in the lee bunk for a snooze.

About an hour after I'd lain down, Bri's hassling with Aquarius on the opposite bunk woke me. I put the water on, ground coffee beans, and watched the two of them bickering. I really didn't want to go on deck. I felt I'd fucked up. The first sip of black coffee with honey helped. I went up the ladder and looked forward.

Bonded loaflike on the sunrise horizon lay land! About three points off the port bow. Land, by God! I drank the coffee, looked, and grinned! Land! The Marquesas! Tears came to my eyes. I couldn't say a word.

"Papa, Aquarius won't leave me alone and I'm hungry."

"C'mere, kid. Did you ever eat with your eyes?" She came on deck. I said, "Look forward there." She looked.

"What's that, Papa?"

"That is a big loaf of bread."

"You're crazy, Papa, that's land." So it was.

Of course, I didn't know *which* of the Marquesas it was, and I really didn't give a damn . . . but I should have. I freed the tiller, trimmed sails, and headed straight for it. I wasn't thinking at all. Before noon, the land still at some distance, squalls were everywhere. Small thunderheads right down on the water. Pouring rain and lightning. We were forced to dodge between them as best we could. They were borne like vessels by the southeast trades. If one got us, it was drop the main and hang on for about three minutes of high wind, cold rain, and bright lightning.

Presently birds were visible about the land looming up ahead. All our eyes were hungry to see something green. Some green growing thing. Greens were scarce; apparently the small island was uninhabited. Sheer volcanic cliffs ran right down into the sea. I broke out the chart for the Marquesas. The chart was spread out on the companionway hatch. I was attempting to orient our position when I glanced over the side. My heart leaped into my throat and panic seized me! It was a terrifying sight! It was bottom! I could see the rocky bottom close under the keel. Paying out the mainsheet and bringing her stern to the wind, I discovered *Sea Lion* would "sail by the lee," that is, with the wind on the same side of the hull as the boom.

In a few breathless moments we were in deep blue again. Though frightening, that shoal water on the north side of the little island identified it on the chart. Fatu Huku. A giant scissor-tailed frigate bird glided close by the mast and put his eye on us. Aquarius freaked at the closeness of land and demanded to be put ashore. Alas, it was not the port of entry.

Had we continued on our original course at the sighting of land, we would have arrived at Nuku Hiva (the port of entry) about now. Now it was necessary to head west-northwest through all those squalls again. It was already past noon when we had our lunch of kipper snacks, cheese, crackers, and raw onion sitting on the engine cover with the frigate bird circling. The bilge demanded pumping.

That sun burned straight down, but the southeast trades disguised its heat. A giant shark slid past the starboard side going in the opposite direction. It rolled on its side and put a glazed eye on us.

By midafternoon there were three of the Marquesas in view. It was a great relief not to have to break out the sextant. Just look at the chart. There was no doubt. We were right there. Those squalls were fierce. It was necessary to give them complete attention.

The minute I let my mind wander to the reception and pleasures that awaited us ashore, one would pounce. The winds inside one of those things were about fifty knots, the rain cold and stinging. Lightning crackled all about. There was never time to reef, just drop the sails and hang on. By nightfall we were in the lee of Ua Huka. It's quite a large island and very little of the southeast trades found their way over it. We ghosted through the night. There were no navigation lights of any kind ashore. There were no lights of any kind anywhere except the white lantern on *Sea Lion*'s stern. This was the third night of no sleep. The bilge needed pumping again and got it before daylight.

By good light we were clear of Ua Huka. Some of the islands I had seen the day before were hidden in mists on the horizon and different ones were in view. By now I was only taking in coffee. Bri was feeding herself on what she could get at. The boom jaws worked well, but they were cutting a groove in the mast. The mainsail still had its L-shaped tear, and the leech of the staysail was frayed.

I studied the chart and determined the best course to arrive at the harbor of Taiohae, Nuku Hiva. Away we flew on a broad reach with the wind on the starboard beam. Somehow I was completely disoriented. We arrived where the harbor should be, but it was not there. I discovered the mistake, came about, and charged back right alongside the island with the wind dead astern. The sun bore mercilessly down on my bare head. Somehow I couldn't find my cap. My brain was numb with fatigue. Now it felt as though it was being cooked inside the skull. Wrapping a wet towel around it helped. There was no leaving the tiller. We were less than a hundred yards off the shore.

With the wind astern, all was strangely quiet. The sea was deep and blue. The shoreline reared straight out of the sea to form magnificent cliffs just as some ancient volcano had spewed them up. In back of the jagged peaks were high mountain meadow swales green with coconut trees, sometimes coming right down to the water at a notch in the vertical volcanic spires.

There was no sign of human habitation. Then came the wall, sculptured to infinite detail by erosion of wind and sea. The history of life was recorded in stone. Hallucination? Perhaps so, but there it was. For more than an hour *Sea Lion* sailed silently along the mural wall that told it all. Unimaginable was the tale! True, I was quite out of my mind.

Bri and Aquarius had fled the merciless sun and captain to the cool, dark mahogany recess of the cabin. I could not take my eyes off that mural. Consciousness expanded to reveal myself looking. It was all there, the story etched in molten stone and the little brown man with bloodshot eyes and a wet-towel turban watching; sailing by in a ragged boat and watching it unfold. Only when the little ragged boat reached the end of the wall did the tale end. It left no memory of the tale. The wall is still there.

Suddenly we were in water the like of which I had never seen. It poppled up in little sputes! All around water sputing up in poppling little peaks! *Sea Lion* yawed first one way, then the other. There was no wind in lee of the wall. Frantically, I prepared to start the engine.

With slack sails *Sea Lion* sidled sideways toward the rocks. I'd leave the grinding starter and dash with boat hook to fend her off. Suddenly she'd yaw about, pirouette in the dancing water, and sidle away from the rocks. The engine would not start. I made up jumper cables to the twelve-volt used for compass light. She wouldn't even sputter. Never coughed once. After an hour of frothing, cursing torment the batteries abandoned the effort.

Cat's-paws of wind leaked over the peaks, and *Sea Lion* fiddled out to deeper water. The farther she drifted, the more cat's-paws caught her. Eventually we were sort of sailing along in the lee of the island looking for the harbor entrance. That entrance is way on the northeast corner, and we arrived at the narrow opening late in the afternoon.

If ignorance is bliss, I was blissful. Without the least knowledge of that harbor's reputation, I pointed *Sea Lion* into the mouth. The opening is very narrow and in the absolute lee from the southeast trades. You couldn't call it beating. It was taking head on giant swirling cat's-paws of wind that slipped over, around, and through the mountain peaks of Nuku Hiva. They came slashing down from the heights to the harbor below. There was no room in the mouth to tack, even if there had been a constant wind. Sense of time left me. It seemed forever that we fought an outflowing current near that entrance. Back and forth, sometimes the wind in opposite directions on headsails and main.

I could see buildings on the opposite shore. A determination set in. The mate and ship's dog were banished from the cockpit. Mighty gusts bounced off the walls of

the entrance without warning. Just as suddenly there'd be no wind at all. Knockdowns quickly became routine. By the time we were far enough in to see the bay, there were rope burns on both hands and a foot.

There was a plastic squirt bottle of pure honey just inside the galley. I grabbed it, screwed the top off, and swallowed several large gulps, pumped a cup of water, and re-entered the fray a total madman! It became evident that the way to handle the situation was to secure both headsail sheets so the sails were pinched in tight. The tactic was to wait for a blasting gust, let it knock her down, hold the mainsheet in tight, and she'd squirt ahead a few feet.

I could see at least three sailboats at anchor. One was a very large black schooner. There were people lining the taffrail. With the inspiration of an audience and another charge of honey, we finally reached maneuvering room where it was possible to tack in the cat's-paws. With the jib and main sheets in hand and straddling the tiller, I had the sensation of driving a wagon and team of mules!

Presently we were within hailing distance of the schooner. They sent a waving cheer. *Sea Lion* picked a spot, and I dropped anchor for the first time in forty-four days. The line payed out while I fumbled at the halyards and dropped all sail. Consciousness was fading. I almost forgot to snub off the anchor line. Below, Bri was sound asleep. Aquarius fled, scrambling ratlike through a portlight, as I staggered into the cabin. The place was a total mess from so many knockdowns. I heard an outboard engine. A young man from the schooner came alongside with the stinking noise. I invited him aboard and below. Words were exchanged. I offered him a cup of wine, took mine, and sat on the bunk. That's all I remember of that day.

# Chapter Five

AWAKENING DID NOT COME all at once. First there were
the eyes. There was an arm with a cup hanging from one
of the fingers at the end of it. Then faintly the sound of
bilge-water slosh and a dog barking. When I sat up, the
arm with the hand holding the cup proved to be mine.
It was absolutely dead. A child was talking. Leaning over
and looking aft, I saw Bri with all her stuffed dolls and
critters arranged about the cockpit. Then recollection.
We were at anchor in a port. The cup fell and rattled
around on the dried stains where wine had spilled.

That arm had to be restored before I could prime and
light the stove for coffee.

"Hi, Papa. I thought you was dead."

"Well, I'm not, not completely."

"Good. We're all ready to go ashore."

I looked at the clock. I'd been asleep twenty hours.
Aquarius was forward barking intermittently at the life
ashore. On deck was the most un-secure tangle imaginable. The sails lay where they'd fallen, except that a great
fold of the main was in the water. Halyards flopped about
in the whispering little cat's-paws. Coffee and honey.

"Briewfn, did you eat?"

"Sure did."

"What did you eat?"

"A little bit of everything."

"How about some oatmeal?"

"Bleck, yuk, no thanks! Let's go ashore."

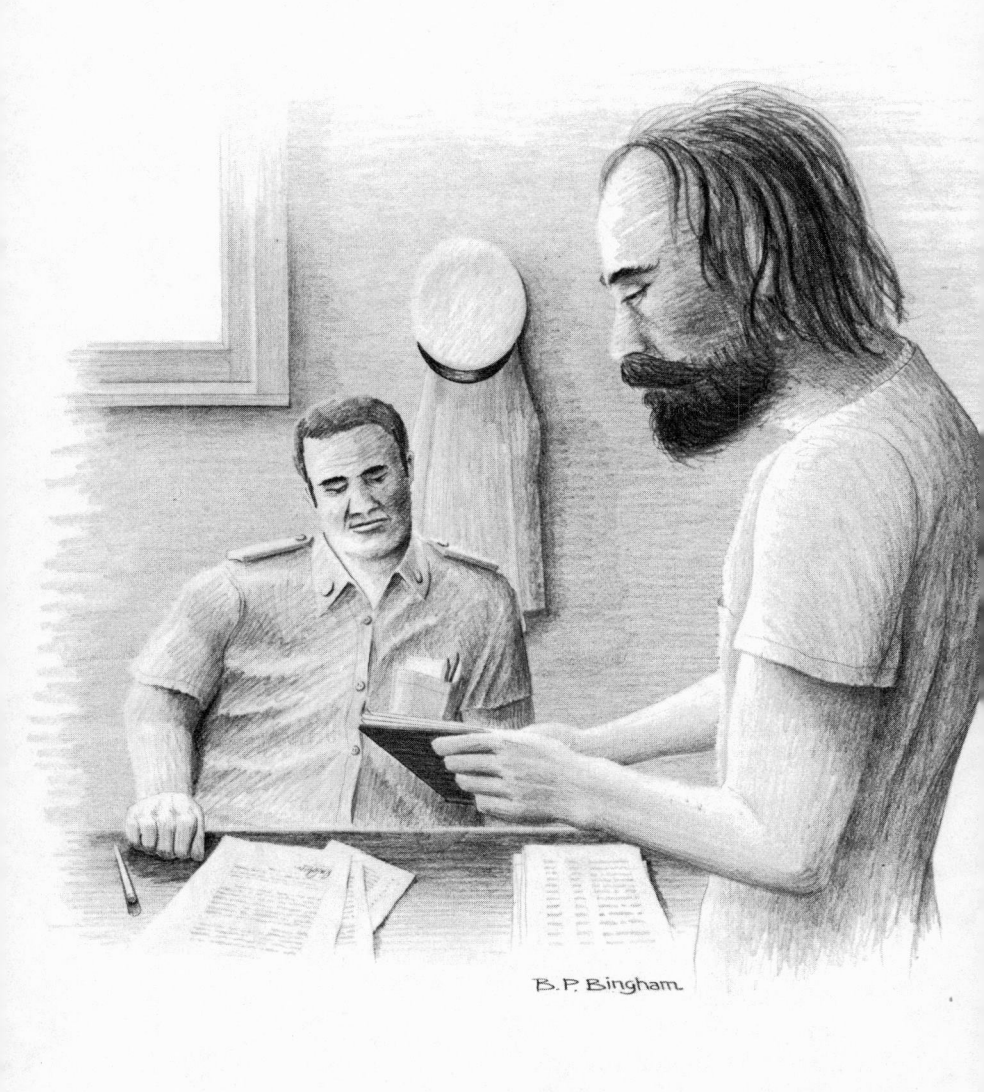

B. P. Bingham

After oatmeal, I brought in the line and spinner of the taffrail log. The total reading was 3,616.7 nautical miles. While I was in the process of tying the sails down, that skiff with the outboard came from the big black schooner. There were two young men this time. One was the same as yesterday, the other an Oriental lad. Aquarius bristled and growled as they came alongside. They said they'd better not come aboard till we had "cleared the port." They also informed me that no one would come out to the vessel for that purpose. I would have to go ashore and find the "gendarme." They invited us to come aboard the schooner after we had cleared port. The schooner's name was *Fletcher Christian.* They would sail for Fiji in two days.

Inflating the dinghy in the cockpit with a foot pump, I studied the shore. It was a movie set. One dirt road came down from the formidable government buildings on a rise to the right, past a concrete pier, around the bay, to and through a tiny village mostly hidden in mango and coconut trees.

"That's enough pumping, Papa. Let's go ashore."

"Relax, kid."

She stamped one bare foot. "I'm the bossterd now! I want to go ashore!" She was in open rebellion. Bri had many words that were her own, words she made up. Like "drump," for both drop and jump. "Bossterd" meant both boss and bastard, with some turd thrown in.

Her life had been hard the last few days and our relationship was at a very low ebb. She was eager to get away from *Sea Lion,* the ship's dog, and me.

With our passports, the bill of sale for *Sea Lion,* and vaccination cards, we departed for shore, leaving Aquarius aboard. I rowed the rubber dinghy to the pier. Bri was already pissed because she could only take one stuffed critter ashore. When we got to the road, she headed straight for the village. I had to stop her. We had a

knockdown, drag out right there in the road before she would come, stiff-legged, up the hill to those government buildings.

No one there spoke English. I was made to understand that "the man" was not about and that I'd have to come back later. We hung around a few minutes, but Bri could not be restrained longer. From the road we could see a commotion of people gathered at a thatched hut near the water's edge down in the village. Thinking I might find the "gendarme" there, we went. Bri was running. She wanted people, the more the better.

As we approached the festive group, I could see that something was being sold at the thatched hut. It was meat. Just before Bri got lost in the crowd, someone tapped me on the shoulder. I turned and saw a native man dressed in khaki shorts uniform. He was very belligerent.

"You come! Now!"

A hush fell on the edge of the crowd nearest us. The man's neck was thick and he had one cauliflower ear. His manner was that of police anywhere. He seemed ready for me to attack.

I said, "Can my daughter stay here?"

He bristled. "No talk! You come! Now!"

I took Bri's hand, and she did not resist. The man fell in behind us and "marched" us back up the hill to the "gendarme."

We were ushered into a formal, military-looking office. "The man" was there. He was French. He offered to speak no English. I could speak no French. I handed him the passports, the other papers. He glanced at them, then at Bri, and put them in the desk drawer and locked it. I knew it was not customary to surrender one's passport. Under the circumstances, I didn't object. I was made to know that there was a man in the village who spoke English and that I should find and return with him.

That man's name was Maurice. He owned one of the
small grocery stores, the only one with a "bar" in the
village. Being of Scotch and Marquesan descent, he did
speak some English. He had been born there and was a
trader like his father before him. Maurice was not very
friendly and obviously considered it an imposition to go
up the hill with me to interpret. But he did go, and this
time Bri was already amongst the people. She had picked
out a jolly fat lady, a native woman, who took great
delight in being chosen. Her name was Hina. Of course
Bri called her "Mama," and that was that.

Maurice and I drove up the hill in his pickup truck.
After stopping to talk with some men where stores were
being unloaded, we arrived at the spartan office.

I could understand nothing of what was being said
between the two. Then Maurice turned to me. "He wants
to know if you have a crew list."

"No. What crew? It's just my daughter and the dog."

More French, and it seemed grave.

Maurice asked, "Where is your wife?"

I blushed and said she had been killed in a car wreck
back in the States. It was not the truth. They just looked
at me and back at each other before the gendarme said
something.

Maurice turned to me. "The dog cannot come ashore.
That's all. You can go now." He left the office and I
followed. He got in his truck and drove off without me.
I was shocked. Some hero's welcome!

By the time I walked to the village, all the meat was
gone. I did manage to get a very large bone with some
meat on it for Aquarius. The people of the village
shunned me. They were polite enough when I addressed
them, but in general they avoided me. It was difficult to
find Bri. When I did, she was at the home of Hina. Hina
and several young girls were delighting in Bri's antics.
The young ladies shied away at my entrance, but Hina

was very friendly and eager to communicate. Yes, Bri could spend the night.

Rowing back alone to *Sea Lion,* I was tired and puzzled. Hell, hadn't I sailed all the way from the States, single-handed? Nobody seemed to give a damn, as if it happened every day and I was the ugliest one in a while!

Aquarius was joyous at my return without Bri, and about turned inside out when he got the bone. I puttered around cleaning the cabin some, and went to bed at dark to the sound of sloshing bilge water. I slept fifteen hours.

When I awoke and swung my feet off the bunk, they landed in a quarter inch of bilge water! Pumping started while the coffee water heated. After about thirty gallons were pumped down the cockpit drains, I made porridge for breakfast. I missed Bri but was glad she was ashore. The truth is I was exhausted after the voyage. We had made it, safely and in good health; wasn't that enough? No. The transom was leaking at least ten gallons a day, at anchor. As water got deeper in the bilge, the leak increased, indicating that the higher seams had received the worst strain. I had to build proper new boom jaws. The ones built at sea were too thin and cut into the mast. The decks were leaking rainwater. The rigging was fraying badly in many places, and the sails needed patching.

It was necessary to get the engine running in case I had to maneuver for a haul-out. Getting in the dinghy proved to be a chore with the kid katchers acting as a fence. Not only could one not fall over the side . . . you couldn't even climb over! They were positively a pain in port. I cast off and rowed the dinghy over to *Fletcher Christian.*

She was an old Baltic Sea trading schooner about seventy feet in length. I was welcomed aboard and met the captain and his wife. The crew were all very young people of both sexes from many different countries. The captain (forgive the loss of name) was friendly and con-

gratulated me on sailing into the port. Yes, they had fresh batteries to start their diesel, and that afternoon when the skiff was free, they'd tow me alongside and get *Sea Lion*'s engine started. No, there wasn't a place to haul out.

Rowing the short distance to the pier, I wondered how it was possible to feel so let down in such fantastically beautiful surroundings. The climate was ideal. Gentle breezes leaked over the mountains carrying sounds of laughter from ashore. All was green, growing, and abundant. On the road I walked listening to the jungle birds talk. I could see that the people of the village were gathering and mingling around the crossroads, where a single road left the main one and ran back through the village and up into the hills beyond. It seemed they gathered there almost daily whether there was a reason or not. They just met, chatted, and strolled about.

From a distance I could see Bri. She was the center of attraction for a small group of mostly ladies. As I drew closer, she and Hina left the one group and were strolling over to another. On meeting, Bri waved at me, said "Hi, Papa," and went on with her hand in Hina's and a smile on her lovely little face. I had in my pocket the last two barrettes to keep the growing bangs out of her eyes. I could not get her attention, and gave them to Hina. The little queen with long blond hair and big brown eyes was being introduced to her smiling subjects. I hardly existed. When my eyes met another's, they turned away. Perhaps it was the beard. What the hell, I had to talk to Maurice anyway.

Maurice's store was two walls with shelved canned goods, one big, wide worn counter, and stacks of bulk and boxed goods piled about the floor. A tiny door on one side led to the "bar," and since he was busy, I went in there, already tasting the first beer in more than a month.

The bar itself was tiny, about three loose stools and nobody behind it. There were three or four tables with odd and mismatched chairs. A Marquesan man slept on one of the tables snoring. I sat at the bar and waited. It was Maurice who finally came and, before I could ask, set an open bottle of Hinano in front of me, grinned, and left. The beer was far from cold, but no chilled champagne could have tasted better. Maurice knew exactly how long it takes a thirsty sailor to down a beer. I grinned and held up two fingers, he grinned, opened two Hinanos, and left.

As I was just reaching for the third beer, two of the crew of *Fletcher Christian* came in from the street door. They sat at a table and Maurice entered. I walked over, and they invited me to sit. One of them was a young lady —from where, I don't recall. Two of those large beers and I was buzzing. The talk naturally turned to sailing, and the young man wanted to know about our passage. He was the first who'd shown the slightest interest. I went blank. I couldn't recall details and just gave him the facts. Forty-four days out of L.A.

There was a great gulf between us. I couldn't understand it. I bought the next round and asked about their passage. They'd come through the canal from the Caribbean and were headed for Fiji to charter. The drunk man snored.

Duty called the two. I finished my beer and went in to talk to Maurice whether he was ready or not. He could tell I was impatient for information and possibly a bit loco. He closed his account book, stopped waiting on the few customers, who were delighted to witness the conversation in a foreign language. No. There was no boatyard or place to haul out. No marine supply store. Yes, Hina was all right to look after Bri. Yes, there was a chain saw, in fact he had it. No, it did not run well. Yes, I could rent it.

I thanked him and left the store. Walking toward the

crossroads, I was confused, angry, and a bit drunk on the beer.

Suddenly I looked up and saw a giant ripe mango hanging from a beautiful tree.

The tree was at the crossroads and was in the yard of another store. I went in and asked if I might have the mango. A Chinese lady took down a tool at the end of a long pole, went out to the tree, and I pointed to the one I wanted. Five cents, please. I was beginning to learn that every fruit-bearing tree belonged to someone.

I went to Hina's house to visit Bri. She was having good times and ignored me, possibly because she feared I'd take her back to *Sea Lion*. No need to fear, that was the last thing I needed.

A squall dumped pleasant rain on the road back to the pier. I ate the juicy sweet mango and let the rain wash my beard.

Rowing out to *Sea Lion,* I thought, "Hell, you don't have it so rough, the ship's dog is quarantined." Once aboard, I broke out the next to last gallon of California wine. Starting the engine would wait. I got drunk.

Early next day the engine started. I ran it sputtering and popping around the bay a couple of times before shifting anchor. This time *Sea Lion* had her bow out to the swells and a smaller stern anchor toward the village. The next day *Fletcher Christian* sailed—I mean motored— for Fiji.

Days were slipping faster. Suddenly I'd have nothing done.

A French Navy ship came into the bay and anchored near the government complex. It looked like a destroyer escort to me. There was bingo for the people, volleyball and souvenirs for the crew. This time when I chanced upon Bri, she ran and hugged my neck, but hurried back to Hina. She had a runny nose and was scratching bites on her legs.

The next day Hina asked me to take her back aboard

because she was sick. She was, too. High temperature, diarrhea, and vomiting. Baby aspirin to get the temp down and bananas to combat the diarrhea. Fresh oranges from ashore for juice and stay in the bunk, dammit! Bri always had a strong constitution. She was seldom sick and mended quickly. She ate nothing but porridge for two days. I don't know what it was, but the natives called it "grippe."

The harbor was getting crowded. *Taporo,* the supply boat from Papeete, was offloading stores with longboats, and a glass sloop named *Brinestormer* arrived with three brothers from Seattle. Last port Galápagos, twenty-five days. Never have I seen such a well-turned-out and orderly rig. The three brothers were the wished-for image of American youth. They even liked each other!

As soon as Bri's fever dropped, it was physical combat to keep her down. She cursed me, but I didn't worry about that—she cursed in English. She insisted on seeing Hina.

I was drinking a beer at Maurice's when a big white schooner entered the harbor under power. I watched through the louvered glass window. She was a pretty vessel. I paid Maurice the exorbitant price for the Hinano and went down to the dinghy to be on hand for their arrival. The vessel's name was *White Squall II.* She flew New Zealand colors. There were three people on board. Ross and Manene were the owners, and there was an English lad. I've lost his name but remember the face and a good hand that goes with it.

When next day I went ashore and met Bri, all her hair was cut off! Not only the bangs to a short bushy scrub but up to her ears all around! I looked at Hina and am sure no language barrier existed. Hina was a simple native lady, perhaps, but what the hell business was it of hers to hack the child's hair off!?

Bri and Manene of *White Squall* had the opportunity to

get to know each other, whether they wanted to or not.

I fell ill. I suppose it was the "grippe," but suspect that suffering injustice was the cause. Whatever the cause, I was truly sick and helpless. It dragged on for feverish days. In the end Manene sent cooked food over from *White Squall,* and the three brothers shared penicillin from their medicine chest. I was on the mend.

Through awkward discussions with Maurice and an ancient wood-carver who lived on the hill, I located the proper wood for the new boom jaws. It was called *hau.* Sort of a tough gum. There was a downed tree at the edge of the village, and I was told it was mine if I wanted it. After tuning up and sharpening Maurice's chain saw, I picked out a thick limb that had the right shape. I sliced the limb in place on the trunk, and no holding device was needed. Soon the two opposing curves in rough blanks were in hand. Maurice said he didn't want any rent for the saw, but I gave him five bucks. He was not the sort of fellow I wanted to get too deeply in debt to.

Now, there was a complete woodworking shop on the island, but it belonged to the government. At first I tried hand-planing the tough, fibrous wood, but the grippe still had its grip, and I implored the authorities to run the two pieces through their planing mill. You'd have thought I'd asked for France's independence. Although I was made to feel like a Mexican dog for the asking, the wood got planed. Rasping and fitting the pieces to the boom took another day, and I discovered I'd have to recess the carriage bolts because they were some short. There was no bit in my tool chest long enough and no sockets to get down in the recess to tighten the nut. The three brothers off *Brinestormer* came through, and the jaws were finished.

Next came a band of copper chafing around the mast where the boom jaws worked. The copper was aboard and it didn't take long. By the time I got to scraping

those goose barnacles off the bottom, most of them had died and fallen off by themselves. Tiny fish were eating away at them.

Eventually all the cockpit seat lids were refastened, the mainsail taken ashore and patched, and a new topping lift spliced.

A French Navy assault vessel came into the bay, anchored near the government complex, and put marines ashore for "exercises." The strange-looking war vessel had a helicopter on a stern deck.

*Mariposa,* a cruise ship, disgorged hundreds of fat middle-Americans, who promptly trampled the flower beds of the houses ashore while poking their Instamatic cameras in the windows.

Four or five "ladies of the evening" met them on the pier in the afternoon. I was sure I recognized some of them as the ladies from Hina's house.

The general ostracism ashore had taken its toll on my psyche. I shaved off the beard. It made no difference.

One afternoon two khaki policemen rowed out to *Sea Lion.* I recognized the one who spoke to be the same who'd escorted Bri and me to the gendarme. This time he was all smiles, but his partner was grim. He didn't disarm Aquarius! They were not even allowed to hold on to the gunwale. We spoke in our broken manner of nouns and hand signs.

Suddenly I realized that they suspected me of having thrown my wife overboard on the passage! I was flabbergasted, but it all made sense. Of course! Who in Nuku Hiva could even imagine a car wreck? I had no crew list, no official sanction, we had simply sailed . . . and who was to know how many had sailed?

From that moment on my whole attitude toward the place and its people changed. I became short of temper. I wanted nothing more than to be away from that harbor, and dived into the work of preparing to sail.

The meat vendors came down out of the hills with sacks of fresh-killed meat on their backs. I had tried their product before. Even the smell of cooking meat turned my stomach. We never had it at sea, and my system couldn't take it. We did stock up and cook some for the imprisoned ship's dog.

We got word that a German couple who lived up in the hills raised vegetables for sale. Bri and I sought them out shortly before sailing.

They did have a good assortment of things growing neatly on a hillside. Their prices were high but it was the only game in town. Much to our discomfort, we also found swarms of *hini hini*—those tiny tropical black flies that lay their microscopic eggs under the skin. Anywhere away from the beach they swarmed. You could not see them and could hardly feel their bite. An hour later a dreadful itching sensation appeared at each bite. A little hard knot forms at the bite and the itching becomes intolerable, even for a grownup. Don't scratch! Ever try telling that to a child?

*Taporo,* or some other supply boat from Papeete, arrived and departed about twice a week. *Brinestormer* departed and *White Squall II* shifted anchor around to another bay.

*Sea Lion* was ready to sail. I went to the gendarme's expecting trouble. I demanded our passports and papers. The month we'd been there had given them plenty of time to communicate with the States, and anyway, where could we go with our leaking hull but to Tahiti? He was pleasant enough and handed over the papers and passports.

Bri threw her departing fit, and we sailed out of Taiohae Harbor under all working canvas on December 17, one month and two days after dropping anchor. In all the time we'd been there, not one vessel had entered or left the bay under sail.

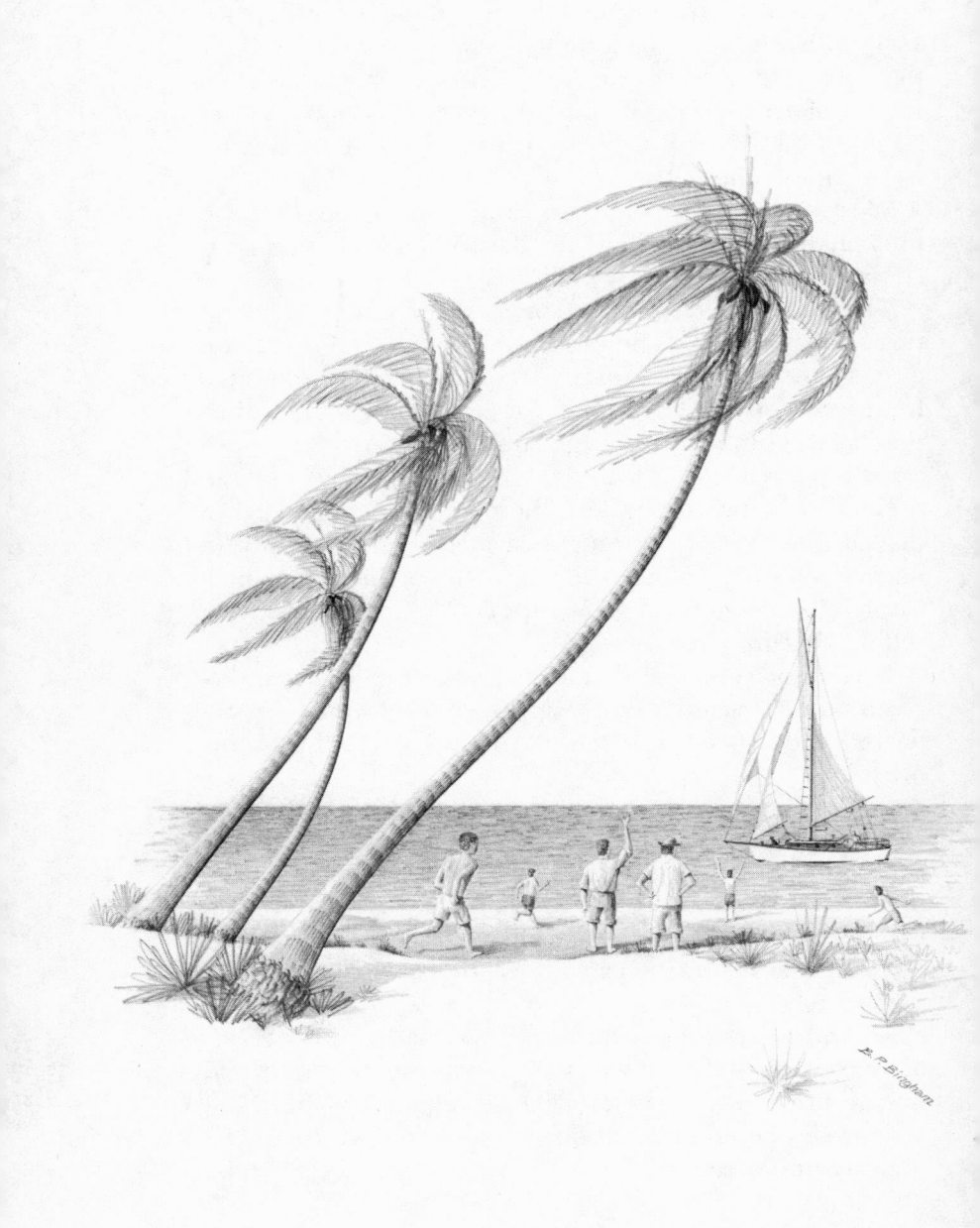

# Chapter Six

IT WAS GOOD to be away. The sail out through that night-mare entrance was effortless. Moments after *Sea Lion* passed through that narrow slot, we were in rollers. Giant eternal rollers set in motion so long ago by the first trade wind. Marching up out of the southeast. The main needed a reef but I left it up out of vanity. We were still in sight of the vessels inside the snug harbor. Once the harbor was down astern, I scandalized the mainsail and payed out the taffrail log spinner.

Not liking the chore of celestial navigation, I had decided to dead-reckon the relatively short distance to Papeete. It is only seven hundred miles. The accepted route through the Tuamotu Archipelago lay between the atolls Ahé and Manihi. That's all I knew about the Tuamotu. I was about to learn a lot more.

It took the first day out to get accustomed to those southeast trade seas. *Sea Lion* rode best with one reef in the main and both headsails sheeted flat. The tiller lashed a bit to weather, and we were flying! No squalls, white puff clouds, and that ever-constant wind. "Really marking it off," as Scuppers, the Sailor Dog, would say. There were long, leisurely snacks on the engine cover. Plenty of "read to me" and "lap time." We were averaging better than a hundred miles a day by the log.

Just when I was thinking we'd found paradise, Bri's sores from scratching the *hini hini* bites got worse. While bathing them with antiseptic, I noticed some little telltale

red lines running from two of the sores up her left arm. They could be indications of blood poisoning.

In the evening of the third day out I expected to raise the sight of Ahé. There was nothing. Not even the lights of other vessels, and the route was much traveled. In the night, warm air from the darkness hinted land passing to port. Sunrise came and there was still no sight of Ahé.

Noon approached. I worried and prepared to take a latitude sight. Once more up the shrouds, hoping to avoid the arithmetic of working out a sight. Land ho! Rather, coconut tree ho! First one coconut tree sticking up out of the sea, then another, and more. Four hours later I entered in the logbook that we were leaving Ahé astern on the port quarter. Still no sight of other vessels. It made me uneasy, and I slept very little through the night. All the next day we sailed in those high, rolling seas with the wind on the quarter. The mate's sores weren't any better, but we'd soon be in Tahiti, where there was bound to be medical attention.

Just before sundown coconut trees appeared off the starboard bow, and I entered them in the log as Rangiroa. The chart said it was a very large atoll and showed a village and port. Perhaps there was a doctor there.

I altered course and studied the pass on the chart. There was a nasty-looking outer reef. At dark we were sailing by the lee well past where the "gate," or pass, should have been. Those rollers were crashing on the reef about fifty yards to port. Fatigue was catching up on me. I took *Sea Lion* well off the reef to north, but still in sight of land.

Joy of joys, I got her to heave to for the first time! It was a thrill. She'd just saw back and forth in those rollers, taking them on the bow, parked for the night. I slept fitfully.

Daylight came and there was no sight of land anywhere. After a pot of porridge and a pumped bilge, *Sea*

*Lion* headed back toward where the atoll of Rangiroa should be. Just before noon the coconut trees appeared dead ahead. The current had set us twenty miles to the north during the night! I shook the reef out of the main. We were beating hard into those monstrous rollers with that coral reef for a lee shore.

It was hard work and damned unnerving, knowing that any rigging failure or serious mistake would stack us on that reef where the big rollers crashed.

*Sea Lion* was heeled mightily on either tack. Bri and the ship's dog went below. Rope burns from the jib sheet had made my hands raw, and fatigue was fought with gulps of honey. Hard beating was letting considerable water into the bilge and I could hear it. Still there was no pass.

Just when it was all becoming unbelievable, it got worse. *Sea Lion* was caught in a wild riptide! A strong current was pouring head on into the wind and rollers. She pitched and bucked and threatened to shake the wind out of her sails. Lashing the tiller, I scrambled up the whipping shrouds and saw a notch in the green line of coconut trees. No outer reef! There was flat, light blue water beyond the notch.

I scrambled down the ratlines, took the tiller in hand, and payed out the mainsheet. Her stern came up to the wind, and she surged into that mighty current toward the notch. Full force of the wind hit the mainsail at right angles, and both headsails strained at the stays. She inched her way up into the current. It was an eternity before the spit of rock- and brush-covered land began to draw up on the port beam. By then the current was whipping out of the notch like a river rapid.

There on the shore to port was a pile of rocks as high as my head and with a weathered and splintered spar sticking up out of it. It was the only navigation aid or sign of human presence.

Suddenly a whip of current lifted *Sea Lion*'s stern, and her rudder came out of the water. Immediately she headed for broaching disaster. I held the lifeless tiller all the way to weather and waited for her spars to be deposited with that in the rocks ashore. Just as suddenly the stern dropped on a whip and the rudder bit back in. She answered the helm and took the next one on the bow.

What a tractor she was, what a forgiving tractor!

Water was turning light green and blue beneath her keel. At an exact point just within the notch that mighty current released her. She spurted ahead into a sea with barely a ripple. God, it was a moment of joy! Fatigue vanished; we were sailing on pure velvet. Just enough wind spilling over the tops of coconut trees to give good steerageway.

Both the mate and the ship's dog were asleep below. *Sea Lion* and I had it all to ourselves. We turned left and ran down along little white beaches and coconut trees. You could have read the headlines of a newspaper sixty feet below! Now not a ripple except her wake as we glided between and around coral columns that rose straight up off the white bottom to within inches of the surface. I climbed the shrouds, and the sight of it all made me very high.

Astern, beyond the notch, I could see the same kind of view stretching away to the north.

There was no evidence of habitation till I saw what appeared to be a blue 1956 Plymouth convertible parked on the beach. We went in closer. It was a homemade outboard boat with tail fins! *Sea Lion* put out for deeper water and a bit more breeze. I wanted it to go on forever, but up ahead the coconut trees ended. Bilge water gurgled just beneath the cabin sole.

*Sea Lion* was looking for a spot to anchor when people came running down to the shore waving. I counted six, four men and two boys. The boys were jumping up and

down with excitement and the men weren't exactly blasé.
*Sea Lion* found her spot. I let the hook go and the line
payed out. The anchor struck forty feet below in a puff
of white dust. The white nylon warp turned from blue to
green with depth. I snubbed the line off; there below I
could see the Danforth anchor dig down out of sight in
the bottom. The sails came down.

We were nearly a hundred yards from shore and a bit
below the thatched huts where the people were waving.
Bri and Aquarius woke when the sails were lowered.
They had gone to sleep with hell breaking loose and
wakened in serenity.

Aquarius leaped, barked, and danced at the shore,
while Bri urged me to hurry with the dinghy. I was anxious too. I wanted to know where in the world we were.

There was no keeping Aquarius out of the dinghy. He
had not set foot on land since he was a puppy. I stuffed
some fishing jigs and a couple of packages of sewing
needles in my pockets. They had been bought in California for trade goods. We rowed straight in toward the
shore as two of the men and a boy walked down to meet
us. They had several dogs with them. There would surely
be one hell of a territorial dogfight when Aquarius got
amongst them. Well, he'd just have to learn. He jumped
into the water and swam while we were still fifty feet from
shore.

Even before the rubber dinghy touched shore, it was
obvious which of the men was the "chief." They both
wore old pants rolled to the knees and shirts with few
buttons, but the chief carried himself in that particular
manner. The minute Aquarius shook the water out of his
coat, he headed straight for the dogs. They scattered into
the brush yelping. Something wasn't right about that,
but I was busy giving attention to the meeting.

Only the chief's and my own stiffness kept us all from
hugging each other. There was no need for language.

The chief immediately invited us to the thatched huts. On the way I gave him the "trade goods." The men held up the jigs, laughed, and thought they were cute.

I had the chart for the Tuamotus under my arm. When we arrived at the huts, the chief ordered fresh coconuts for us. Men climbed the trees barefoot, nuts fell and were husked. The ends were knocked out of a few, and we drank the sweet water. The rest filled a tow sack. They were all captivated by Bri. The two boys couldn't take their eyes off her, yet they could not play as children; they were already grown workers.

The dogs didn't behave anything like dogs. They ran crying and hid from Aquarius's friendly advances. He wanted to play; they didn't know how. He was sleek and spirited compared to them. The men watched him in awe. Their scrawny dogs reminded me of yard chickens that live only off table scraps. That observation was close, though I didn't know it at the time. Tuamotuans eat dog. It is a main source of protein.

The chief caused me to understand that they were all copra workers. He showed me the pile of drying coconut. They had come from a neighboring atoll in the two outboard boats pulled up on shore near the huts. It was a bachelor work camp. The chief indicated that he had never seen a yacht in this atoll. The others agreed. Finally it was time to ask the embarrassing question. Where was I?

I rolled the chart out on the ground and we squatted around it. Before I could say a thing, they all began to "Oohh" and "Ahhh." They got excited. It was apparent that none of them had seen a chart of all the northern Tuamotu. It was the relationship of the atolls that seemed to astonish them. Then the chief noticed the compass rose. A great clamor went up, and he sent for his boat compass. It was stowed safely in one of the huts. The compass was in a small box and had two headings

written on a piece of tape in the lid. It began to dawn on me that perhaps they had to return to their own atoll and take a new heading to reach any of the others! Perhaps that's the way their employers wanted it. The compass rose printed on the chart had two sets of numbers, one for true and one for magnetic. While they were jabbering and arguing about the rose, I took a pencil from my pocket, one which I'd brought to write down my location, and marked out the true numbers, leaving only the circle representing magnetic. An "Aaa-haaa!" escaped the chief's throat, whereupon I signified the question, "Where am I"?

He immediately pointed to an atoll on the chart. It was Toau. More than ninety miles south of my dead reckoning position. I gave the chart to the chief.

The moment he understood that the chart was his to keep, it was lifted out of the dirt, dusted gingerly, rolled, and stowed with his compass in the hut. Damn good thing I noticed a heading for Tahiti, because I never saw that chart again!

I had given the chief a real gift. He let me know that anything he had or controlled was mine for the asking. All I could think of was sleep. Still in the afternoon, I rounded up mate and ship's dog, and, with the bag of fresh coconut, rowed back out to *Sea Lion.*

Before I could sleep I had to pump the bilge, and before I had finished that all four men and the boys launched one of their boats and came out for a visit.

They tied to the stern, and I invited them aboard. For the first time I'd seen it, *Sea Lion*'s large cockpit was full! Bri was the perfect hostess and reminded me of Manene on *White Squall.* They were having a great time and took note of meaningful things. To them, even in her ragged state, *Sea Lion* represented luxury. There was a little red wine left in the last gallon bottle. I pumped some water in it, and we all had a taste to sip. They marveled at the

stove, and I had to show them how it was primed and
lighted. The compass was more modern and larger than
the chief's. The foam-rubber mattresses knocked them
out. They were most interested in the engine and could
not believe that it would not start. I had to show them.
Fatigue made it hard to keep abreast of their interest.
The bit of wine hurried it on. I made "sleep" signs to the
chief. He hustled them all into the outboard, and they
parted for shore in a light from the most glorious sunset
I had ever seen.

A big batch of spaghetti for us and the last of the
cooked Marquesan meat for Aquarius. I slept the sleep
of the dead, while just the other side of coconut trees
seas crashed on reef.

Sunrise was even more spectacular. It fairly flamed up
over the waving palms as though blown roaring out of
the east by the trades. With coffee in hand, I watched the
growing glow while sitting on the rail. Bri slept on.

The whole atoll was a basin of life. Frigate birds soared
and octopus ghosted along the bottom. There was not a
ripple on the basin's surface. The anchor line was slack.

Bri woke, and we had pancakes for breakfast. Aquarius
kept a barking watch on the shore. He had coconut for
breakfast. He loved it and would have eaten the whole
supply. Before noon three of the men and a boy headed
out toward us in the outboard. They were all smiles and
tied their boat to the taffrail.

They indicated that I should watch and went to fishing.
They used handlines of heavy monofilament. The hooks
were quite large. The sinker was a chunk of coral tied
about a foot above the hook. The bait was large hermit
crab. Laughing and chatting, they'd break open the shell
of a hermit crab, put the meat of its body on the big hook,
and throw the rig over the side. It never had time to get
anywhere near the bottom, and *whang!* . . . the man
would be pulling hand over hand with all his might. A
very large and strange-looking fish would break the sur-

face and land in the boat. No two fish were exactly the same, but they were all large and strange-looking. More than once only a head would come into the boat; a shark had got the rest. They'd cut up the head for bait, and that worked just as well as the crab.

Using an old spark plug for a sinker and tying on the largest hook aboard (and half the size of theirs), I asked them for some bait. They were delighted and tossed a double handful of hermit crab into the cockpit. I never saw anything like it! Every time I threw the line in, a fish hit it, and I caught either a fish or its head.

In Nuku Hiva I had heard that some species of fish in the South Pacific were poisonous. Each time one came up, I'd ask by Mexican sign if it was okay to eat. Yes. They were all good. When their boat was damn near full, they cast off for shore. I filleted our catch, breaded, and fried them. We feasted!

Bri's sores were healing and seemed only to flare up with lack of sleep. Another one of those Tuamotuan sunsets and yet another glorious rising! Somehow I felt trapped in paradise. Perhaps it was the thought of how long it had taken to get out of Taiohae. The specter of that pass into the atoll was always in the back of my mind. The beauty of the trap held me. We rowed ashore to find hermit crab. I had no intention of bothering the men hard at work ashore. Up and down the water's edge Bri and I searched while Aquarius scuttled in and out through the bushes. We found not one crab.

I had given up and figured we'd had our last meal of fresh fish when the chief and another came upon us. They were sweating from the gathering and splitting of copra. They were short on patience. I was made to know that hermit crabs could be gathered only at noon, which time it was, and under one particular kind of bush. Once they were sure I had the message, they left as abruptly as they had come.

Under the proper bush were huddled hundreds of

hermit crabs. After filling the ship's bucket, we rowed back to *Sea Lion.*

Once aboard, Bri went straight for the staysail boom, which she used to play "horsie." At best it was a patched, tired stick and promptly broke under her bouncing weight. Add one day.

With the staysail boom replaced from stock on board, we set about shifting anchor. Since the day before I had noticed that the anchor line was fouled around a coral head. Only the chain was in contact with the sharp coral, but it was necessary to kedge by taking another anchor out in the dinghy. I had to get in the water to unfoul the line. With face mask and flippers I kept one hand on the dinghy and a sharp lookout for sharks. I saw none.

With the anchors aboard we sailed gently toward the pass. It was Christmas Day, 1970. We anchored near that notch to study its habits.

Once *Sea Lion* was properly secured to the bottom, Bri said, "Let's go ashore, Papa." I put together a picnic lunch and, with the ship's dog, ashore we went.

At this point the coconut trees ceased and the vegetation dwindled out into bushes, then to rocky coral. There was a very large tide pool and I expected to find an easy meal. To my surprise, there was no life of any size in the pool.

We discovered why in the small stream that led to it. As we were about to wade across, a patrol of sharks filed past. The tide pool must have been their restaurant.

I was standing there watching them slide by in water not much more than knee-deep, when Aquarius jumped in and paddled across. They paid him no mind. I picked Bri up and waded across. The sharks were not the least interested in my legs.

We found a spot in the lee of a coral bluff and sat down in the bright sunshine to enjoy our Christmas picnic.

"Papa, what is Christmas?"

"Well, it's Jesus' birthday."

She finished a sweet pickle. "Papa, who is Jesus?"

"Well, he's been dead a long time."

"Yeah, but who is he?"

"He was a man who changed the world."

"If he's dead, why does he still have a birthday?"

Now this child wasn't yet four and I was in trouble. "Listen, kid, we gotta get back so I can pump the bilge."

"No. I want more Christmas."

What the hell, the vessel wouldn't sink and she was sure having a great time.

Presently she asked, "What did the world use to be like?"

"Well, there was mostly lyin', cheatin', and stealin'." I was afraid I knew what her next question would be, and it made me sad, for I really didn't know that the world had been changed for the better, if at all.

"Papa, did Jesus like little kids?"

"Well, now, he sure did! By all accounts, he sure did like little kids."

That satisfied her, and I could tell Jesus was all right in her books. We finished the lunch and picked our way around to the windward side. The southeast trades had slacked some and the breakers on the outer reef weren't so ferocious. In fact, I could see much exposed coral inside the breakers. I made plans to go out there for lobster while Bri was asleep that night. Going back to the dinghy, I picked a path that would be easy to negotiate in darkness.

From aloft a complete view of the pass was laid out for study. There is no tide in the Tuamotus. I had to figure out what caused the water to move through the pass. It wasn't flowing out so rapidly as when we'd entered.

I had put off really cleaning the bilge, just pumping off the excess for days now. It was beginning to stink badly. First I pumped it down to where it was manageable, and

took up all the cabin sole boards. Then, with bucket and sponge, I set to work. The stench gagged me. That stagnant water had turned the floor timbers and the keel black. There was an awful gas rising with each spongeful. What a way to spend Christmas. At least it was done. I left the boards up to air the bilge and went back up the ratlines.

According to the departed chart, coconut trees only grow on the windward side of the atolls. There were no mango or banana trees and all the coconuts were owned. The west, or lee, side of those great circles of coral reef were barely awash with no vegetation at all. It became apparent that if the wind shifted a bit south, more of those rollers would break over into the basin below the coconut trees. It had to get out somewhere, and that was the pass.

I had noticed debris and driftwood ashore indicating that sometimes there were storms out of the northwest. What must that pass be like then!

We got to bed late that night because Bri said, "Read where the Sailor Dog sails to Christmas." To protect sanity, I'd taken to modifying the tale with each reading.

When quite sure the mate slept soundly, I took the flashlight and a burlap bag (tow sack), and sneaked ashore in the dinghy. To get to the outer reef, it was necessary to wade across the thirty or so yards of still water. It was spooky. There were holes and mounds, but the flashlight beam cut through the clear water.

On the reef itself the walking was easy. I wore knee-high rubber boots. Presently I saw two tiny red coals glowing in the light beam. I simply walked over and picked up the lobster! It was more than a foot long. I stuffed the critter in the tow sack and wanted to look for more, but worry of what might happen if Bri awoke and found me gone prompted a hasty return.

Once aboard, I tied the lobster in the burlap bag to the

taffrail so the creature was just under the water. Fine refrigerator.

In the morning while coffee water boiled I went aloft. The wind had shifted ever so slightly east. Water in the pass appeared to be without movement at all. Now was the time to sail . . . but there was no bread on board. I broke out the cumbersome Dutch oven. The sea biscuits were numerous but not excellent. My mind was on the pass. The current appeared to be flowing in. I had even forgotten the lobster. Thought of waiting for the oven to cool angered me. I threw the damn thing over the side, hot Pyrex glass shattered, and it sank to the white bottom.

By the time I had the anchor aboard, the current was definitely flowing into the pass. It was obvious from aloft that the deep water, about twenty feet, was close to the point of land where we had anchored. The distance between coconut trees in the notch was at least a quarter of a mile, but light-colored water told of shallows on the north side. With the wind about forty-five degrees on the starboard bow, we tried it. No good. The incoming current and leeway would set us in the shallows.

There wasn't room to let her fall off and jibe around; we had to come about properly.

The second time I cut closer to the shore at the deep-water side, but still ran out of room before we cleared the notch. On the third try we got a good long run at it from the still water inside, damn near scraped the starboard side on the land, and we made it!

We were out of the pass and sailing away north with the wind on the starboard quarter. Once we cleared the trees and outer reef at the north end of the atoll, *Sea Lion* really flew! The water was glass flat and there was plenty of quartering wind. We were bound for Tahiti!

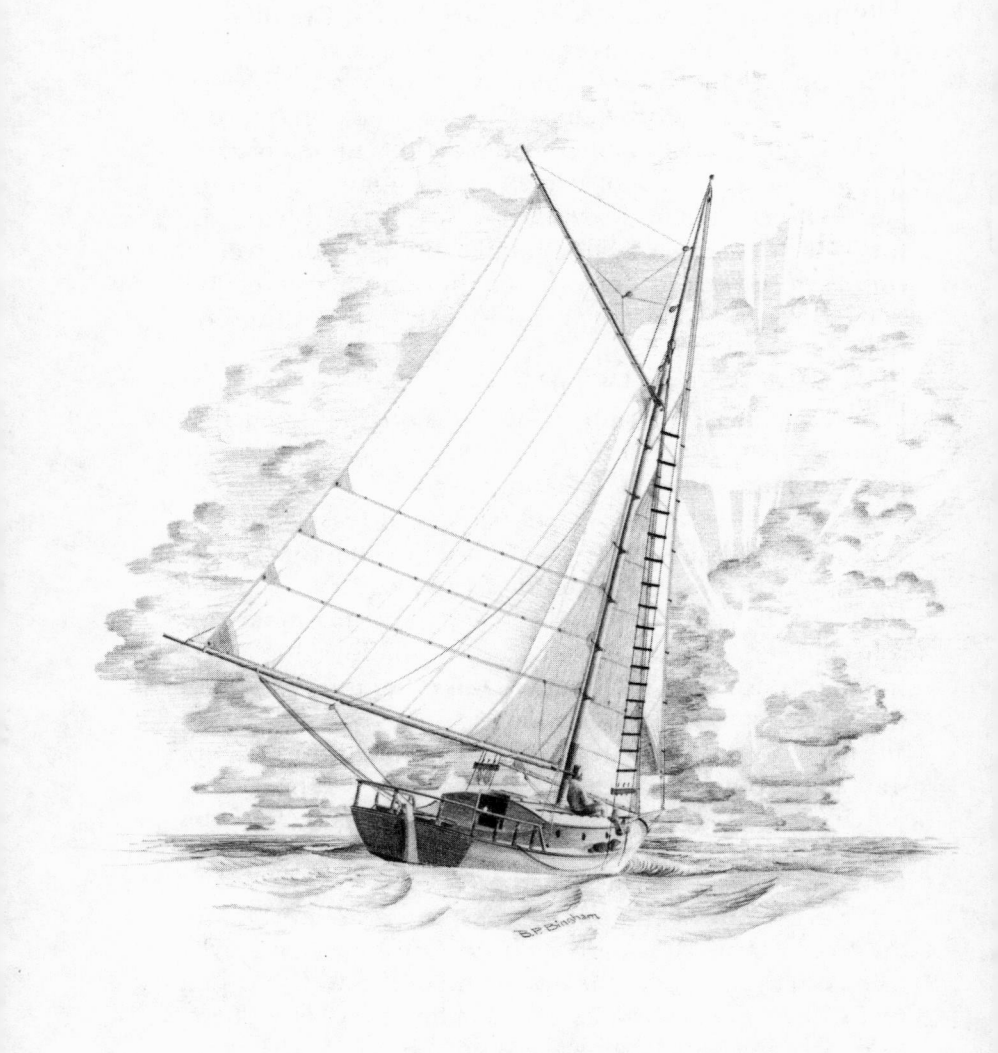

# *Chapter Seven*

IT WAS SUNDOWN before *Sea Lion* ran completely out of
the lee of Toau and those flat seas. Southeast trades were
borning new rollers. We feasted late on fresh lobster. I
slept in comfort, knowing we were well out of any shipping lanes.

The sun, rising, noon, or setting, was always at least
spectacular in French Polynesia. The next morning it was
glorious! Wind had freshened to a good Force 5 and *Sea
Lion* was really marking it off. Aquarius had grown so
much he could no longer enter the portlights without
great difficulty. Still, he refused to enter by the companionway ladder.

Making a "landfall" in the South Pacific is not what
one might think. I mean, you seldom see "land." In the
daytime tops of islands are almost always covered by
clouds. What you see is a faint hard line angling up from
the horizon, then another line angling down out of the
cloud.

That's the way Tahiti showed up shortly before noon.
The only way you can be sure it's land is that it doesn't
move. Tahiti lay dead ahead. I pointed it out to Bri, and
the three of us sat for hours on the foredeck watching it
grow. Soon green appeared. Then patches of cultivation
in different shades. By late afternoon we could distin-
guish smoke from settlements near the shore. We were
passing the northwest end well off the port beam by
sundown. Wind died as we drew into the lee of moun-

tains. Before midnight Point Venus was slipping by three hundred yards to port. I wished we had stood off for the night, but *Sea Lion* was making steady progress and we were in no danger except from fatigue.

Presently the glow of electric lights loomed up off the port bow. That would be the harbor and city of Papeete. There were huge ground swells and little wind. Soon harbor entrance lights were off the port bow . . . they were not "red right returning." We wallowed over the swells, rising and falling as on an elevator, past the lights, and into the harbor. There was a system of range lights for entering the harbor at night, but I did not have the key. Sleep was after me again. I took *Sea Lion* lazily off out of the way to starboard.

Suddenly surf was breaking! To starboard. Then to port. Surf was breaking all around. There was no wind to maneuver. Help! Drop the anchor and sails at the same time. The anchor line ran out. We had little way on, but the line ran and ran. The flashlight showed white surf breaking everywhere except astern. I pulled in the slack till the anchor line felt firm. It was practically straight up and down when I secured it. The beam of light showed her stern to be hanging over coral not five feet down. I watched awhile; nothing happened, so I went to sleep. It was just a nap. Up and drinking coffee by first light. *Sea Lion* was parked in a notch of coral heads.

First the sails went up and flopped loose in the light airs. The anchor was at least a hundred feet down, straight down! With it aboard and with the aid of the boat hook to fend off the coral, we cleared the notch. I sheeted in the sails and *Sea Lion* gathered steerageway.

Papeete is a big deep-water port. I was trying to figure out the buoyage system and sail in the fitful breeze when a tugboat bore down on us. No doubt he was headed for *Sea Lion,* so the sails came down. There were two men on deck. The tug came about and alongside. Without a word

of "by your leave" or even hello, they threw a line with an eye in the end.

If there is anything bad about boating, it is being towed. It is a helpless feeling. There is no control. What the hell, I didn't know where to go anyway. The eye went over the samson post and we bore away for the inner harbor. Those deckhands knew their work and had *Sea Lion* snubbed up close against puddening on their starboard side.

I was totally unprepared for the unfolding scene. We were heading straight for downtown Papeete! Presently a row of sailboat masts appeared. Apparently their sterns were tied to the main street! We came to a slot in the row of boats. The tug came smartly about, and I was ordered to drop the anchor. I did so and the tug backed down, then called for their line. I threw it to them while we were still backing down. They let go of *Sea Lion*'s stern and departed. *Sea Lion* was gliding backward into the slot.

A small knot of people had gathered on the concrete wall. Obviously they were off the other sailboats. Just as I was about to throw a line ashore, one came sailing out. It landed across the taffrail and started running into the water. My toes grabbed it and the line in hand flew. A plank was shoved out, and I lashed it to the taffrail. Bri came on deck. You should have seen her face light up! People! "Where you from?" "How was your passage?" "Anything you need?"

It was a busy afternoon. The "man" came and cleared our papers. No one asked about my "wife." I was even led to believe no one would see if Aquarius went ashore. The local newspaper took our picture.

Fabled Tahiti. As ridiculous as it was, I liked the place on sight. Even the wild car traffic noise off our stern wasn't personal. Briewfn was thrilled. Aquarius freaked. We were on display along with the rest. The quay—"key" as it was called—was a major tourist attraction.

Poor *Sea Lion* was a ragged mess in the lineup. Most of the vessels flew their colors. There were no flags on board *Sea Lion.*

Our gangplank was a limber two-by-six with no handrail. Neither Bri nor Aquarius dared attempt it. Great! For a while at least I could go and they could not. I took Bri onto the quay to let her run, but did not want to rub the ship's dog's presence ashore in the face of authority —at least not the first day. It was December 29.

The mate was brought back over the gangplank kicking and screaming. I was asleep by dark, but she hung on to the bustling activity ashore late into the evening. Bri was a candle fly; leave a light on, or anything happening, and she would not sleep.

I was up early and slipping ashore before anyone on board knew it.

I found a cup of coffee. The first someone else had brewed in a long time. It was delicious. Still before daylight I strolled the "key" and surveyed the vessels tied there. There were twenty-seven. It was apparent how long which had been in port by the landlubberly articles on deck. Some were growing potted plants. At least a third were from the States.

With the first rays of sun the street began to buzz. There were hundreds of Vespa motor scooters. Cars of every make and model blew their horns and jockeyed for position. There was no sign of traffic control anywhere. Exhaust fumes were overpowering. By the time I arrived at *Sea Lion*'s gangplank, the traffic was a roaring, screeching, bashing bedlam! Bri woke when I jumped down into the cockpit. She loved it and could hardly wait to get in it.

To bathe, one simply went up onto the quay, selected a hose, and turned on the faucet. You just lathered up right there with the traffic scant feet away. The only privacy was your bathing suit. Bri could not wait. Aquar-

ius jumped and freaked when he was left aboard. The bath was refreshing. Water out of the hose was warm and soft as rainwater. The air was about seventy-five degrees.

Some of the boats had families, and there were children of all ages for Bri to play with. All the little ones like her were naked. I left her on the quay and went aboard to try and get *Sea Lion* squared away. It was the "kid katchers" that made her look like one big Irish pennant.

I longed for liberty ashore, but when you're single-handing, there's nobody else to take care of the grubby details. The harbor was a big, sprawling place, and I had to find a boatyard to haul out and locate the marine supply stores.

The quay was already Bri's domain. She ran and squealed from hose to hose like a hummingbird. There was always someone hanging about to keep an eye on the kids while I scouted.

There were three possible places to haul out. I picked the old established one with a marine railway. Ellicott's, it was called, but there was a big new sign that said it was a division of Rockwell International. The older Ellicott was always about, but one of his sons ran the place. It had a major drawback. It was located all the way around the bay. I'd have to have some kind of transportation.

Returning from a scouting foray, I was informed by Henry on *Challenge,* the boat to *Sea Lion*'s starboard, that Aquarius had fallen in the water trying to get ashore. Seems a certain Bernard had rescued him and put him back aboard. It was obvious from Henry's reverent attitude while mentioning the name of this Bernard that we had been paid an honor by having the ship's dog rescued by such a personage. His vessel was pointed out to me. It was an impressive steel hull ketch named *Joshua.* It was anchored all the way at the end of the lineup and far enough out to require a dinghy to get aboard. Very exclusive.

Late that same day I came across the Lambretta scooter. It was a battered and ancient vehicle that had to be push-started. It was registered to no one and its license plate simply read "Yacht."

Seems the old scooter had passed from vessel to vessel for years and the standard price was fifty dollars. It was in the hands of a jolly Englishman before it passed to us. Now we could really get around. Bri rode standing in front of me holding to the handlebars.

That evening we were introduced to *poisson cru*. Just before dark three different catering vans showed up in the parking lot near the quay. We just followed the crowd from the yachts and my cooking days were done! They served a paper bowl filled with a sort of salad made from raw fish marinated in lime juice. French bread slices served as edible spoons. One could also get a sweet fresh chilled coconut with a straw stuck in it. The fish was fresh local tuna. It wasn't cheap, but there were no more dishes to wash!

The days of waiting for our appointment to enter the yard were spilling into each other. Living was easy. Easy but expensive. I wanted to run into this fellow, Bernard, to thank him for saving the ship's dog. I was told he was writing a book. There was some tall tale about the man having sailed singlehanded around the world. Nonstop. By way of the three Great Capes. For unknown reasons I was prepared to meet a pompous snob.

When it did happen that we met, he was one of the most sensitive, intelligent, and likable persons I had ever known. His name was Bernard Moitessier. He dismissed the saving of the dog and complimented me on the "kid katchers."

Quite often in the evenings a group of people off the yachts would gather around a bottle of wine on the quay just to swap sea stories. This night it was New Year's Eve. We all stayed later and the stories were taller than usual. Still, I was in the bunk asleep before the new year

arrived. Just after midnight there was a great splash and surge that woke me. A Fiat had roared off the street and hit smack between Henry's *Challenge* and *Sea Lion* with inches to spare! The Fiat's hood was under *Sea Lion*'s stern and bumping her bottom. There were plenty of drunken Tahitian revelers about, and half of them were in the cockpit. Others dived in and smashed the rear window, which promptly let the car sink. A very inebriated lady opened the driver's door and bobbed to the surface. She was handed up, sputtering, into the cockpit and *Sea Lion*'s mainsheet was thrown in by someone to tie to the car. Trying to save the mainsheet, I broke out the nylon warp, and it too was tied to the car. The drunken lady managed to tell the staggering Tahitians that she was alone. About twenty Tahitians pulled the Fiat back up onto the quay and I went back to sleep. Bri never even woke up.

We had been in port four days, and I figured it was time to stop cleaning up after the ship's dog. At the first crack of daylight I took Bri's hand and then carried Aquarius across the limber gangplank. The animal was ecstatic. He jumped and danced and wiggled and waggled. There was a park across the double boulevard, but Bri and I started walking along the quay. There was no traffic as yet, but one car did flash by fast.

We heard a loud *thump* and yelping behind us. The first car Aquarius had ever seen had hit him! He had been heading for the park. I made Bri stay where she was and ran back.

Aquarius was lying in the road yelping and couldn't get up. Thick blood ran from his nose and mouth. He had been run over right across the middle and his back legs didn't work. I picked him up off the pavement and took him to a hose. As I washed the blood off he was going into shock. I took him aboard and laid him in the cockpit. He was very still.

One wouldn't expect to find a pet vet in an area where

some folks still ate dog. I didn't. Aquarius lay where I had
put him for two days. Just a glimmer of life showed, but
on the third day he had dragged himself down into the
cabin to escape the sun. It was the first time he'd ever
used the ladder. We got him some raw meat from the
local supermarket, and that third day he ate.

The time had arrived for us to haul out in the yard.
With the help of jumper cables and ether, the engine
spluttered to half-life and lines to the quay were let go.

Measurements had been made and a cradle awaited
*Sea Lion* on its little railway car. The rails led up out of
the water to a turntable where a choice of spurs radiated
out from the circle. A couple of the spurs were occupied
by near derelicts that some hapless soul was paying stor-
age on. The yard in general was trashy. Old dry rot
timbers lay about and the toilet didn't work. That does
not mean it was cheap. Nothing but the sunshine is reasonable in Tahiti.

As she sat up in the cradle, *Sea Lion*'s gunwale was
twelve feet off the ground. A long ladder gave access. We
fixed Aquarius a bed under the keel, but he didn't like it.
He wanted to be aboard.

The first things to go were the "kid katchers." They
had never caught anything but stuffed animals, a couple
of cushions, and one bird. They were completely disas-
sembled and rolled into balls of nylon small stuff, thus
becoming very valuable.

The next thing to go was the engine. The main boom
was used as a crane to hoist it over the gunwale and
deposit it on the ground. Work was done alone. That
started a marathon of changes for *Sea Lion*. Once the
engine was out, the real work began. Those through-hull
connections had to be properly closed. The shaft log
plugged and the apertures in sternpost and rudder filled
in. It wasn't done in that order, or any other order.

Much of the time was spent chasing parts. On one such

trip I found a rare thing in Tahiti, a good buy. It was a big fisherman anchor at less than a dollar a pound. With the crown on the scooter's floorboards I had to look around the shank to drive back to the yard.

Next to leave the vessel was the toilet. Then the attendant sealing of its through-hull fittings. All work was done properly. At least as properly as available materials would allow.

Warren Ellicott, the son, found me an ancient Tahitian caulker. I ripped out and cleaned all seams he thought necessary. Other than the entire transom, those seams he picked were mostly along the chine. He was a craftsman. In the mornings he'd often bring us fresh fruit when he came to work on his old bicycle. I felt as though my grandfather was helping me make the vessel seaworthy.

Bri missed the quay. When suppertime came, we'd climb aboard the Lambretta and head for "poisoned crew." Sometimes it would be raining and she'd duck down behind the scooter's shield. She loved that ride; it was a real "goose-me."

The distance being about three miles around the harbor to the quay, we'd often stay after supper to visit wherever the wine bottle was.

I recall one pair on board a small sloop named *Hobit*. They were both young schoolteachers from California. He was tall and thin, she short and muscular. Oh, did we laugh and cry!

Bri's day in the yard was something to behold. The place was a minefield of booby traps. She avoided them all, getting filthy in the process. There was a litter of tiny wild kittens. In and out under band saw and planing mill she chased them. Of course one was weaker and slower than the rest.

I was down in the cabin cutting out the stainless counter top to make a place for the stove to gimbal when

I heard her coming up the ladder. "Papa, Papa! Look what I got! Come here!" Then I heard a sickly *thwap.* I looked out into the cockpit and there she was at the top of the ladder with a string in her hand. The other end of the string was down in the cockpit tied around a dead kitten's neck!

I raised hell, but none of the Tahitian workmen in the yard would admit to tying the string around the kitten's neck, yet it was a perfect square knot.

I had given up trying to keep clean clothes on her and bought a dozen pair of bikini bottoms. All that was necessary was to hose her down at night. The mosquitoes were very bad in the yard and she still scratched the *hini hini* bites from Nuku Hiva. Soon she was a mass of sores from fingertip to toes. It wasn't unusual; all the young Tahitian girls had great scars on their legs from infected insect bites.

At first I treated the sores by washing her whole body in disinfectant. Antibiotic ointment was put on each one and each covered with a Band-Aid at bedtime. The sores got worse. She scratched incessantly. One day I washed her off, dried her down, and wrapped her from ankle to wrist with three layers of gauze. No medicine. Then I went over the gauze with two layers of masking tape, leaving only the armpits and crotch open. Go ahead and scratch, kid.

The mamas on the quay came down on me. They spilled out dire predictions of atrophy, and so forth. I left her in the mummy suit for five days. All the mamas were up in arms about my treatment of the child's condition. On the sixth day I removed the tape and gauze. Not a sore was to be seen. They were all healed.

Soon Bri picked out her "family." There were lots of kids. At least two were near her age. The father was French and Tahitian and the mother was Chinese. He owned a small boatbuilding yard on the same road down

to Ellicott's. They were Seventh-Day Adventists and delighted at being chosen by Bri. At first it was one night "sleeping over," then two in a row, and soon the whole week.

Within a couple of weeks Aquarius was climbing the tall ladder to get aboard. His back legs still weren't right, but he was getting around better all the time. To get down the ladder, he used it as a slide. He guarded the vessel with a ferocity that astonished the yard workmen. Any tool accidentally left within ten feet of the keel was safe through the night.

Aquarius was a very pretty dog. Away from *Sea Lion*, he was bright and loving to all. One day a young French lady who was crew on a charter ketch named *Mylis* asked me to give him to her. I did so and was greatly relieved.

Within a month I had on my hands a dismantled sailboat on dry land. I worked from daylight to dark seven days a week. No project started was finished in sequence. There was a general unavailability of many things. I sent a desperate order for things from the States.

The jolly Englishman I'd got the Lambretta from was working on a boat in the next yard. He and his lady were cruising in their own boat, paying their way by working on others. We had coffee breaks together, and I learned much from him. One thing I learned was that the family Bri was staying with wanted to adopt her. For a couple of weeks Bri had grown very distant the few times the lady brought her down to "visit Papa." Her absence was needed to concentrate on the work, but I certainly didn't want to give her away. Anyway, they hadn't asked *me* yet, so I kept working and watching Bri's action when I did see her.

One day Bernard came over to the yard and showed me how to make a self-steering vane for *Sea Lion*. He was one of the first people ever to make one. His explanation was so exact, so without pretense, that I understood

immediately. Not only how to make one for *Sea Lion,* but the whole principle. It is very simple if you have an outboard rudder; if you don't, best stay in port anyway. Everything else was dropped and work started on the vane. It was made from galvanized water pipe, plywood, and a couple of broom handles. All the materials cost less than fifteen dollars.

When it was finished, I invited him back to inspect it. He approved. I named the vane Jane and prayed it would work.

That package of things I'd ordered from the States arrived. It took two days to get it out of customs. The airmail alone was thirty-seven dollars. Our money was going fast.

Right on top of the package was seam caulking compound for the deck! You'd understand how exciting that is if it did not exist. Then bronze screw nails of several sizes. So many goodies! At the bottom of the box waited a big disappointment. I'd ordered two-inch drain fittings and hose for the cockpit. They sent inch-and-a-quarter. They were useless.

I'd been waiting for the bronze screw nails to finish the transom. A "V" path was planed flat and clean across all the plank on the outside. Two one-inch-thick by four-inch-wide boards of quarter-sawn clear fir were fitted so the bottom of the V fastened into the sternpost and the tops into frames at deck level. Ample resorcinol glue was applied, and the screw nails through all planks and the ends. The planks on that transom were not likely to move again. It was not a handsome solution, and could not easily be recaulked, but it was done.

I bought an enormous kerosene Primus burner to boil out the gasoline tank. The tank was a round forty-two-gallon galvanized container made to fit *Sea Lion.* By filling it a quarter full and adding detergent when the water boiled, I was able to convert it to use for fresh water.

The engine lay on the ground and in the way until a Tahitian came along and asked for it.

A big chunk of mahogany was liberated from the scrap pile. It was nearly three inches thick, but not big enough for closing the propeller aperture in the sternpost. I made Bri a toilet seat out of it and cut the hole in the shape of a heart. An old-fashioned enamel slop jar fitted in a bracket underneath. At least it wouldn't leak seawater into the hull.

For cockpit shade I bought a heavy-duty English tarp, twelve by eighteen feet. Three spreaders were fashioned from two-by-twos with a section of copper pipe in the middle for ferrules. The tarp went across the boom, and the spreaders held it at least two feet out over the sides. It reached from the mast to a foot past the stern. It was a magnificent tent and could be stowed where the engine had been.

That giant hold where the engine had been was a precious acquisition. I fitted it with a sole. Also replaced the flush engine cover doors with a coaming and hatch that could be secured from below the companionway ladder.

The stove was recessed down into the counter top and gimbals were made by hacksawing the gearbox shifting bracket in half. When two three-eighths shackle pins were removed, the stove could be lifted out with one hand for thorough cleaning.

If I should run out of anything to do, there was a new area where paint and varnish remover could be applied. I bought it by the five-gallon bucket.

I worked as though possessed. Nobody got in my way. *White Squall* came into the yard and left almost before I knew it. Each morning at daylight the fear would mount that this great pile of unfinished projects, once a sailboat, would never again float. Worse than that, if it did someday float, my daughter would by then have been spirited away.

Once when the lady brought her for a visit, I got Bri to sit with me for a talk. I asked her what was wrong.

"Nothing's wrong, Papa."

"Why don't you ever want to come see me?"

"There's no kids here."

"Well, you could at least come and spend the night sometime."

"Yeah, and sleep by myself. I hate *Sea Lion.*"

"Okay. You go along with 'mama' and I'll work on that."

She was glad the talk was over and hurried to the lady, who stood with arms folded, waiting.

Bri had always wanted to sleep in the same bunk with me, but there was not enough room. I had a plan.

By fastening notched one-by-four stringers along each side of the cockpit boxes, fitting cross slats of one-by-fours to the notches, I had a platform frame. Then I bought a sheet of three-quarter-inch plywood and sawed it in sections to fit the cross slats. When it was finally all worked out and fitted properly, I screw-nailed and glued the cross slats to the plywood and painted it all white.

It made four panels that, when in place, formed a strong flush floor at cockpit seat level. The whole cockpit became a bed seven by nine feet. At sea the sections would go in the hold along with the awning tarp.

I hung a large mosquito net from the awning spreaders, put both bunk mattresses under it, and bought three different pretty colored pillows. I called it the "sultan's bunk." The next time Bri was forced to come by to see papa, papa would be ready for her!

She didn't come right away, but I sure slept in comfort. After more than a month of tortuous solitary labor, the mechanical things were about finished. The propeller aperture had been plugged by a big chunk of *hau* wood, fitted and toenailed into the sternpost with long, square boat nails. The same worked for the notch in the rudder.

When they had been puttied and painted, you'd not be able to tell she ever had an engine.

The image of a new vessel was starting to form in my feverish brain. I'd lie exhausted in the "sultan's bunk" at night, but unable to sleep. For sure it would not be a wooden vessel! It would have great beam. The cabin would be aft where the comfort was. Once the process of imagining had started, every hull I saw, every example of rig, and any book that fell into my hands was held in the light of that image. From the first that vessel's name was *Libra.*

With the construction and modifications on *Sea Lion* completed, painting and preparation for paint stared me in the eye. God, she was ugly! She was to be taken down to bare wood from masthead to keel, and too many places had been started to let me change my mind.

On top of it all, I was sick. Very sick, and I blamed the *poisson cru.* Still, the scraping and sanding went on. No power tools were used to remove the old paint, neither did I burn it. With the disk of very coarse grit made for a disk sanding machine I scoured away at the bottom. I could taste copper through the mask. Often I had to drop everything and run to the water's edge lowering my pants on the way. Often I didn't make it.

The sicker I got the slower the progress. One day Bri was brought by, out of Christian charity, I suppose, and, being a bright child, she could see I was sick.

I showed her the "sultan's bunk." She loved it! Much to the dismay of the lady, Bri spent the night with papa.

Apparently it was the first night she had not been mosquito bitten in a long time. Her sores were getting bad again, and her bangs were newly cut. Early the next morning the lady and all her kids were there with candy to take Bri away. She went, but was back on board by nightfall.

I quit going to the quay for "poisoned crew" and

ate French bread and cheese only. Still the diarrhea persisted, and I ran a temperature every night. No medicine worked. It began to occur to me that the cause just might be fear. Fear of being trapped forever in that backwater yard. When an animal is scared, it "dumps" and flees. I couldn't flee. Just blindly plug away and get less done.

One night when Bri was sleeping over with her "family," I rode the Lambretta over to the quay just for company. Aquarius was there and was very happy to see me —why I'll never know. His legs were working well, and he was very popular along the quay.

There was a new face around the fried breadfruit and wine. He was a young giant from Southern California. He wasn't new to lots of the others, but I had never seen him. Arriving as crew from Hawaii a year before, he hadn't found passage farther on. He said he'd be over in the morning to give me a hand. Imagine that!

He was there, too! Bright and early just as he said, and I put the coarse sanding disk in his hand. He pitched right in to scrubbing great clouds of copper and red lead off the bottom. I took new heart. Perhaps *Sea Lion* would float again! His name was Zeke. He had a full beard and an open face. We struck a bargain. If he'd stay to see *Sea Lion* in the water, I'd sign him as crew to Rarotonga, Cook Islands.

He'd been waiting a year for a sailboat berth and was delighted. We both pitched in with zeal. I caulked deck and he removed paint. Within a week the bare wood waited for colors. Blue and gray.

Bri came and went pretty much as she pleased. She liked Zeke and enjoyed his teasing.

The mast and spars were light gray with the masthead knob dark blue. The ends of gaff and boom were also dark blue. Molding on the cabin was blue with the sides a bit darker gray than the spars. Taffrail and gunwale

molding blue and light gray topsides. She was ready for bottom paint.

The moment I saw a chance to flee, the diarrhea stopped. First she got two thick coats of red lead that had to dry three days each. There was a super-duper new plastic bottom paint available in Trinidad Blue for only fifty-two dollars a gallon. I went for it. In fact, two.

The waterline was moved up four inches and Zeke started putting the paint on while I made arrangements to settle the yard bill.

I went by to see the father of Bri's "family" to tell him she'd be sailing soon. They had grown very attached to the child, he said, and were sorry to lose her. But he smiled.

Launch day came. I was concerned about fore-and-aft trim with the engine gone and had paid attention while putting aboard stores. With water tanks topped up to eighty-four gallons, she sat on her cradle waiting to roll down the rails. She was a thing of beauty. Chocks were pulled and the cradle released.

I was on deck and felt the first buoyant moment. God, it was great! She bobbed ducklike and answered to the lines ashore. We moored her to the standby buoy near the railway, and I scrambled into the dinghy to get ashore and see her trim.

She sat in the water square to the world! *Sea Lion* was alive and beautiful!

Hurriedly we finished provisioning the vessel for sea. The day before sailing there was a large box of foodstuff on the back of the scooter and another between my feet. As I was trying to put it up on the stand, the scooter fell over and the hot muffler put a bad burn on the top of my foot and ankle. Excitement at the time let it go hardly noticed.

I returned the scooter to the jolly Englishman, but he kept the fifty dollars.

*Sea Lion* was ready to sail, but the French authorities were not to be hurried. It took another whole day to clear the port. Bri was aboard but not excited about sailing away from kids and candy.

The little sloop *Hobit* was up on the rails, and my teacher friends took pictures as *Sea Lion*'s main went aloft. We were streaming from the buoy in a nice breeze with a coral seawall directly to her stern and the shore a short distance to starboard. All sails up and fluttering, sheets in hand, I sent Zeke forward to cast off the buoy and shove her bow to port.

As the bow fell off the buoy I pulled in the sheets. *Sea Lion* sort of squatted, then lunged forward. She gathered momentum on the starboard tack till our reverse course would clear the seawall. I brought her stern up to the wind and we sailed by the lee down to the harbor entrance, turned right, and flew out of Papeete on a broad reach.

It was late afternoon, March 17, 1971.

# Chapter Eight

As we came out of the lee of Tahiti's mountains, the wind drew aft and freshened. I let the vane, Jane, find the eye of the wind, set the setscrew, and released the tiller. That's all there was to it! It worked to perfection the first try. I couldn't take my eyes off it. As *Sea Lion* tried naturally to come up into the wind, Jane turned the rudder, the tiller moved up to weather as though the ghost of my own hands were on it. *Sea Lion* went back on course, and if she threatened to go past to jibe, Jane moved the tiller to leeward. Thanks, Bernard! May you always have a dry lee bunk!

Soon the full main was too much for Jane to handle, and we had to tuck in a reef. Zeke had told me he was an experienced sailor. I worked from the mast aft and he from the tip forward. When the main went up, the after half of the reef points were tied around the boom! It had to be redone before the sail was stretched completely out of shape.

We were bound for Huahiné, an island one hundred miles west of Tahiti. I had asked about on the quay for the best place to rest a spell. Zeke had been there on the copra boat and agreed that it was the least developed of the Society Islands.

The wind abated with nightfall. I left the reef in and played with Jane. We were in love. I found that when I put a shock cord to take the "lee bounce" out of the tiller, she would hold a course within three degrees! At

least in those seas. Here was a simple marvel of the ages that had to wait before coming into being. Wait till the crews of sailing vessels were reduced to one. Jane stood a twenty-four-hour watch, neither eating nor sleeping, and bitched not!

Around midnight I woke Zeke and turned the very informal watch over to him. I caught a nap, and Huahiné was on the horizon by midmorning. For breakfast we had what anyone would call a giant batch of pancakes. Zeke still looked hungrily at the skillet after the last one was gone. He weighed over two hundred pounds and stood tall for windage. Wherever he walked about on board, *Sea Lion* changed trim.

As we entered shoal water off Huahiné, the new blue-green bottom paint took on an iridescence in the clear, light blue water. God, she was beautiful! We entered the pass in Huahiné's outer reef shortly before noon and let the cat's-paws fan us to anchorage. *Sea Lion*'s stern was tied to a coconut tree, and we went ashore for the customary clearance with the local "gendarme." I suppose cops have to put up a nasty front for all comers, but it sure is disconcerting.

The small port village was as charming a place as you'd hope to find. We saw no tourists. Each time the copra boats came and went was "trading day," when everything from local farmers could be bought: pineapple, vanilla beans, sugarcane, and watermelon.

Zeke had a schoolteacher friend on the island. He arranged that we meet a friend who had a banana grove and pamplemousse trees. Pamplemousse are giant grapefruit. The skin is green when ripe. Each segment is three sweet spoonfuls!

We brought aboard three full stalks of mature bananas and three tow sacks full of pamplemousse. No charge.

The local people didn't eat the fruits from trees and sea. They ate canned corned beef and instant rice.

Whether the fault lay in their eagerness for convenience or the fact that every tree was owned by someone I do not know. The result was the same. Their teeth rotted out by the age of twelve and resistance to infection was low.

After three days I decided to take *Sea Lion* down to the south end of the island. We had heard about a secluded anchorage inside the reef.

The coconut tree line was let go, anchor pulled, and *Sea Lion* started picking her way through the coral heads under sail. The wind was anything but constant. I climbed the shrouds and directed Zeke at the tiller. Many coral heads lay scattered in our path. More than once the signals were crossed and her keel crunched across coral. It was a hairy experience.

The distance was only four miles, but it was late afternoon before we arrived at the anchorage. It was worth it. We dropped the hook a scant twenty yards from an apparently virgin shoreline. The cockpit awning went up, and Zeke dived with mask and flippers to inspect the bottom for damage. Just some lead scraped off the long keel. It was Saturday, and I felt we were at last a long way from civilization.

Protected by the giant tarp from sun and showers, I lolled about the sultan's bunk all the next day plucking bananas from a stalk hanging from the boom.

Zeke rowed Bri ashore. She cavorted naked along the beach where I could keep an eye on her. Zeke had a Hawaiian sling fishing spear. He made claims about its meal-getting qualities, but that whole day he never surfaced with a fish.

Late in the afternoon I decided to give the spear a try and discovered another major drawback to living in the tropics of the South Pacific. There are certain times when certain kinds of coral bloom when the water is poisonous to any break in the skin. That foot with the muffler burn

flared up almost on contact with the water in the bay. Great blisters appeared that filled a cup when drained!

We all three slept in the sultan's bunk, and there was no need for a mosquito net that distance from shore. By Monday morning I was sure we'd found paradise. Suddenly a big diesel engine fired up ashore! Blue-black smoke rose from the greenery, and bushes quaked when the engine roared. We all jumped in the dinghy and rowed the short distance. Just beyond the beach through bushes and trees, a road was being built. A big caterpillar road grader answered to a grinning native's hand.

The hope of ever finding that unowned coconut tree with a stream running under it grew dim.

Zeke learned from the operator that the road was for the expected boom in tourist traffic when the jet airport was completed at the north end of the island. I didn't go ashore there again, but we did go out to the reef. Bri knew we were going, and I waited till she slept. Zeke and I rowed out to the reef; that is, Zeke rowed. My foot was somewhat better and was wrapped in gauze inside the knee-high rubber boots. When finally we arrived at the reef, Zeke was exhausted. I charged off along the reef with flashlight and tow sack. Almost immediately I spotted the two red coals of reflection. I scooped the lobster up and put him in the bag. He was the only one.

There was a great variety of large shellfish literally covering the reef. I gathered a good sampling of all while searching for nonexistent lobster. The tow sack was half full when I returned to the dinghy and we cast off for the distant *Sea Lion.* Zeke bitched and moaned till I spelled him at the oars.

Next morning Zeke went ashore and found a papaya tree. Evidently it was visited by natives as often as the reef. He brought back two green ones. I boiled the lobster and picked off all the succulent white meat, then diced the green papaya and cooked it with the meat in

coconut water. It was nothing short of incredible! A great pot and every spoonful was devoured. Sweet pamplemousse for dessert.

There was a native trick to get the bananas to ripen in order. One half of the stalk was let set in seawater for an hour. That half came ripe ahead of the rest. We ate a four-foot-long stalk in a week.

With the noise of diesel and the rapidly depleting stores, I figured we'd best be on our way to the Cook Islands. The foot was a painful appendage, and I sat at the tiller with Zeke aloft on our way back to the pass. We didn't touch bottom once.

On March 27, we cleared the pass at Huahiné, and before dark the south end of Raiatea was off the starboard beam.

There was a long, rolling swell from the south that I couldn't explain. The wind east about Force 3, the weather generally good, but large thunderheads were all about.

The second day out I got a noon latitude sight that put us at 18°20′S. But I had to guesstimate the longitude, for we saw the sun no more.

It should have been a seven-day run down to Rarotonga. By the sixth day we were somewhere near trouble. The wind kept shifting, and Jane followed the shift. I'd awake to find Zeke asleep, the taffrail log fouled, and the heading changed, for how long I knew not.

Soon the dead reckoning was meaningless and the sun wouldn't shine. I refused to set formal watches because of that dislike for playing captain, yet it was rapidly becoming obvious that a "captain" was needed for Zeke. It was like having two babies on board. The big one ate everything in sight.

I had taken to cooking mostly beans and corn bread. Zeke loved beans, and it was the only thing on board in sufficient bulk to stave his hunger. One try had definitely

shown me never to let him near the galley. His talents for cooking were zero.

In addition to that, he was extremely clumsy, and I was afraid to let him go forward to handle sails. Once he was sitting up on the lee rail and fell off backwards. I happened to be close enough to grab him by the hair and pull him back aboard.

By the eighth day I was beginning to take the general aggravation personally. I wouldn't let him sleep in the cockpit while I was on watch. Everything he did or said irritated me, Bri took his side, and our combined bean gas rendered the whole area radioactive.

Zeke was worried. He kept seeing land in the cloud formations along the horizon and insisting we steer toward them. Perhaps he sensed the bean supply was dwindling.

On the morning of the ninth day out I spotted land but didn't say anything to either of those two about it. Zeke was suggesting rationing our water and food. Bri kept asking, "When are we going to get there, Papa?" The land was unmistakable now, and I changed course to the northwest. Although Zeke fussed about the course change, he didn't see the land. Finally happiness was too much to hold, and I pointed out the firm lines rising and descending from the clouds. We all became joyous and took a hot bath in the now ample fresh water. We felt much better and the island grew before us.

Now that we didn't need it, the sun came out. The land was farther than it appeared. It was late afternoon before the low outer reef showed breaking white on the northeast side of the island. Children were playing in a schoolyard and came running down to the water to wave. The place was lush green and beautiful in the late-afternoon sunlight. *Sea Lion* entered Avatiu Harbor just before sundown. I picked a spot by the dock and dropped the headsails. A gentle breeze came off the seawall that served as

a dock. With the mainsheet in hand, we came alongside with hardly any way on, and Zeke simply stepped ashore with the bowline. I let go the mainsheet and tossed him the sternline. We were secure at sundown.

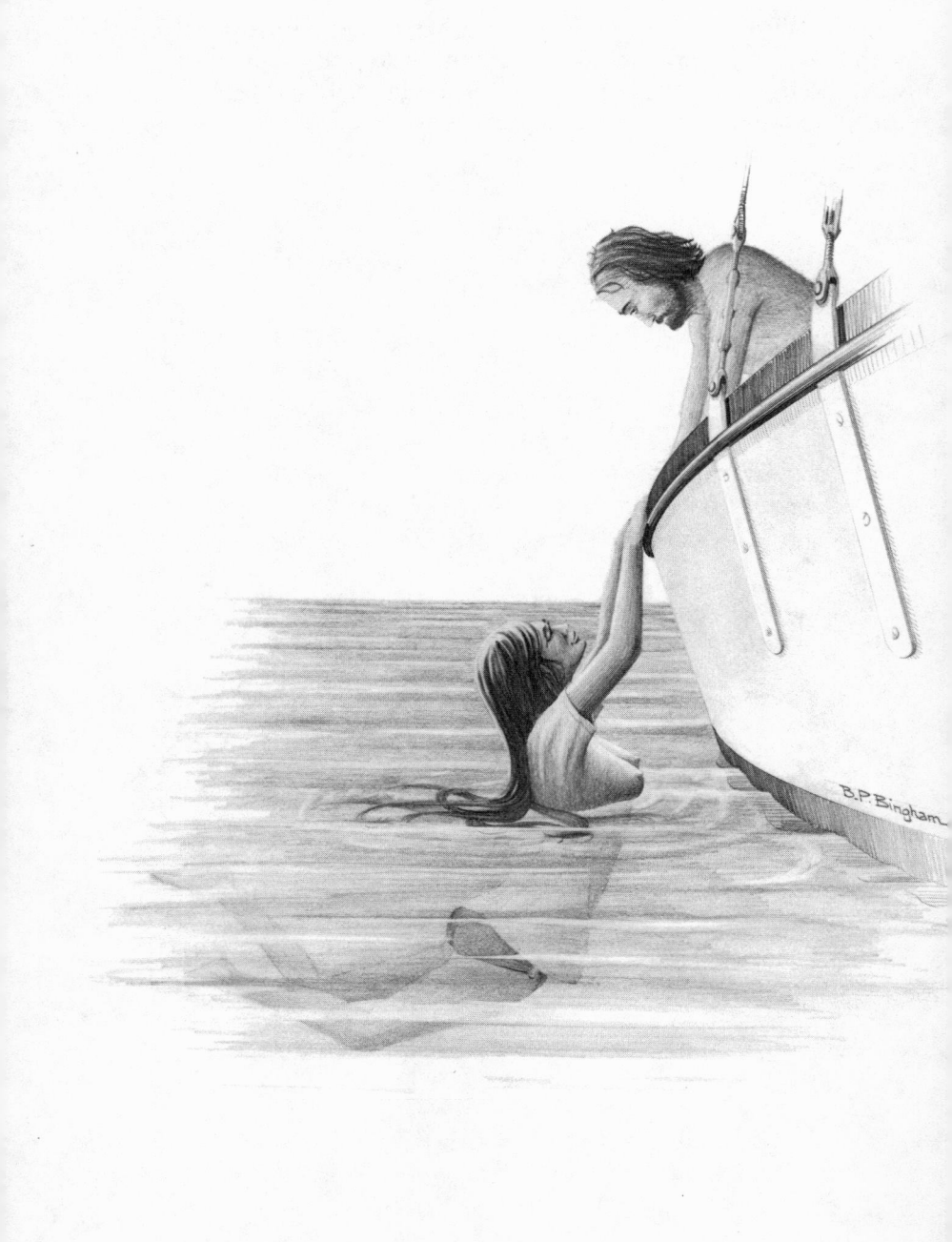

# Chapter Nine

THERE WAS NOT a lot of activity on the dock, and no one seemed to notice that we had arrived. Construction equipment and piles of dirt and materials lay scattered about the area. After waiting half an hour and facing the prospect of cooking supper, we went ashore looking for a restaurant and the port authorities.

We found the authorities before we found the restaurant. Rather, they found us. The three of us were standing at a counter talking to a pretty young native secretary at the Port Office when a Land Rover roared up and slid its brakes just outside. Three native men in uniform piled out. They marched in, and it was obvious we were the objects of their mission. In the strangest English I'd ever heard, the one with the most elaborate Limey uniform, addressing Zeke, demanded to know who was the captain. I stepped forward and was informed we were all under arrest and to get in the Land Rover immediately!

Cramped in that English contraption, we were driven at high speed back to *Sea Lion*. We were deposited on board and told in no uncertain terms not to leave the vessel till further notice.

The spaghetti water was coming to a boil when a friendly-looking young man walked up to *Sea Lion*. He was a New Zealander and worked at the jet airport that was under construction. I told him what had happened and asked him what he thought the trouble might be. Seems that the Cook Islands had recently been given

their independence from New Zealand. He said I certainly shouldn't quote him, but their newfound authority often caused strange behavior in their effort to exactly mimic their predecessors. He said we shouldn't worry, but to be careful, for they had a mean jail.

We finished off the spaghetti but didn't set up the sultan's bunk. Morning came and we had porridge. It was near noon before the Land Rover returned, this time with only one man, the one in the least ornate Limey uniform. He was polite but firm and informed me that I must write a letter to the proper authorities as to just why we went ashore without clearing the port. He would return for the letter later. I felt like a bad boy. I broke out the typewriter. It was the first time it had been out of its case. The first draft was conciliatory. "I am sorry I have been a bad boy." The more I thought about it the more forceful each draft of the letter became. "Where is your quarantine anchorage? Why were we not met at the dock? For your information, in the French ports it is *required* that the captain go ashore to find the authorities," etc., etc. I ended the letter by saying I was sorry I'd been bad. Late that afternoon the Land Rover returned, and the officer seemed very impressed that the letter was typewritten. I asked him if there was a lawyer I might speak to. He did not read the letter in front of us but put it into a very official-looking folder. He took our passports and vaccination cards and put them in the folder, too. No, we could not go ashore till this matter was settled. He would ask about the lawyer.

Briewfn was hard to keep aboard. What did she care for rules? There were all kinds of people walking about there ashore and all she had to do was step off the boat. She simply wouldn't understand and gave me a very hard time.

Zeke was another matter; he seemed very satisfied to remain aboard, where his meals were served to him. He

was beginning to refer to *Sea Lion* as his home! Across the harbor I noticed the hull of a large sailing vessel hauled up on shore. As I watched it through the day, an old man puttered about working on it. It was of old design, possibly an English cutter. It appeared to be in bad shape, but the old man kept at his work. I wondered if he didn't need a hand, a big strong lad, perhaps with a beard, and experienced at sea.

We went to sleep that night still not knowing our fate. The next morning, quite early for officials, two returned in the Land Rover.

From the first word their whole attitude was changed. They handed us our passports, gave us permission to go ashore and enjoy our stay, apologized for the inconvenience, and asked me not to contact a lawyer or say anything more about the matter.

Well now, ashore we did go. It was quite a long walk to what there was of the town. There was no restaurant. There was a clothing factory on the way that made slacks and sports shirts. The stores had all New Zealand products. New Zealand money was the coin of the realm. That's where I first saw canned butter. There was a cannery somewhere that produced citrus juices in large cans labeled "Raro." A tiny public market with only stalks of bananas for sale and a lovely old rambling tropical hotel. I went in and found the bar closed. No, it wouldn't open later. Yes, it was the only bar on the island. Seems the head honcho, one Prince Henry, had been making a speech in the hotel dining room, and so many of his audience left for the bar that he had it closed . . . till further notice! I sure wanted a beer.

Zeke took off on his own to reconnoiter and, walking back to *Sea Lion,* Bri and I met our first priest. He was riding a Honda motorbike and stopped for a chat. He was an impressively friendly individual, and I wish I could recall his name. He told me where the liquor store

was. It was on past the harbor toward the new airport, and by the time we reached *Sea Lion* I needed a rest from walking on land.

We hadn't been aboard but a few minutes when a young native lad showed up. He seemed to be a bit drunk, though he was only about fifteen. He was all smiles and very curious about the vessel and its rigging. I asked him where we might find some fresh papaya. He said to follow him. Grabbing a tow sack, Bri and I did. We walked down along a dirt road inland and presently came to a tall papaya tree . . . in the back yard of a house. He told me to wait on the road and went for the tree. He was about halfway up toward a large ripe fruit when someone hollered and threw something at him. He dropped to earth and ran. We caught up with him farther down the road, and he said we'd have to continue beyond the houses. His English was very broken, and he told me he came from one of the outer islands in the Cooks. I asked him what he'd been drinking, and he told me it was homemade beer and that all the ingredients were available in the stores.

Presently we came to three papaya trees standing in a clearing with no houses about. He climbed the first tree and took the bottom two fruit. One was stone ripe and the other turning. They were as big as footballs! With five papaya the tow sack was full and all I could carry. As we were returning, he informed me that he had just got out of jail. He said they put him in jail quite often. I asked him what for, and he said, "To beat me." He was a bright lad and not given to smart-aleck answers. I said, "What did you do for them to put you in jail?" He thought for a moment and answered, "They want me to change to Rarotonga ways." Once back aboard, I thanked him for the fruit. He called himself Tutai and asked if he could come back tomorrow. I said sure. He smiled and walked away quite sober.

Zeke returned in time for supper, empty-handed. He said he'd met some pretty girls and had been invited to a dance later that night. If he hadn't been so big, I would have thrown him into the bay.

I don't know what time Zeke returned from the party, but he was asleep in the cockpit when I woke up at daylight. I just had one cup of coffee and left before Bri woke. The old man was already at work on the cutter when I walked up.

"Do you need a hand?"

"Sure do."

"Well, I got just the right man for you."

On the way back to my customary second cup of coffee, I met the friendly priest coming along on his motorbike. He told me about a harbor around the northeast side of the island called Ngatangiia. I didn't think much about it at the time and thanked him. When I got back aboard, Bri was pestering Zeke and they battled like two mismatched mongrel puppies. I made pancakes. After breakfast we shifted our place forward along the dock to be more out of the way of traffic.

About midmorning I was lying in the starboard bunk when a tremendous *whack* hit the bottom of the boat! I rolled out and scrambled topside. Bri and Zeke were watching men swimming in the bay and bringing small fish up in their teeth. There was another explosion. They were shooting dynamite in the bay under the pretense of working on the harbor; the real reason was for the schools of small mackerel that had entered the harbor. We put on face masks and flippers and went over the side. The blasts stunned the fish and they wallowed about in profusion. One only had to reach out and grab them as they floundered about. They were good eating too. That went on for a couple of days while I daily praised Zeke's qualities to the old man. Tutai brought a stalk of bananas, and I wondered whose yard they came

from. The explosions were hardly noticeable from shore but in the boat it felt as if someone were dealing great blows to the hull with a big hammer.

Finally the old man consented, and I told Zeke that I had found him a job. You see, the priest had told me no one could remain in Rarotonga without a job. Zeke was enraptured with sailboats and the old cutter was truly a classic. I took him over and a tentative arrangement of employment was agreed to. Zeke went to work but remained aboard *Sea Lion.* I reminded Zeke that our agreement was completed. He was in the Cook Islands, had a job, and should find a place to live. He didn't seem to be in a big rush about moving.

The dynamite shocks to the hull had me worried nearly as much as Zeke's continued presence on board. Bri hadn't picked her "family" yet. I decided to shift anchor down to the little harbor the priest had told me about. After a bus ride down there on Saturday to scout the place, I was excited. It was a lovely spot with a small uninhabited coconut grove island on one side and an old church with its extended grounds on the other. When pronounced by native tongue, its name, Ngatangiia, has a delightful, lilting sound.

Bright and early on Easter Sunday we sailed out of Avatiu Harbor for the solitary anchorage. We had to beat against easterlies, and I practiced navigation with a morning and noon sight. The fix worked out to confirm the land in view. About midafternoon we entered the narrow, deep pass with a beam wind and one reef in the main. There were people in bright-colored clothes about the church grounds. Bri took one look at them and went below to dress up. Zeke was forward with the boat hook and I had the tiller. Just through the pass the clear water became shallow. There were mounds and canyons plainly visible. We picked our way down near an ancient underwater stone-wall fish trap where *Sea Lion* found a

"basin" with about four feet of water under her keel. There was no real flow of current, but she wouldn't stay in her basin with one anchor. I rowed the big fisherman out toward the pass and the small Danforth stern anchor off the port bow. With three anchors she still skittered about, so we put a quarter-inch nylon line to a coconut tree on the little island. Once she was secure, I told Zeke that was it. He'd have to move ashore. He agreed, but a couple of days passed before it became a fact. We put up the awning tarp and assembled the sultan's bunk. Almost immediately young kids came swimming out to greet us.

The girls were very forward with their intentions, and I feared I might never get Zeke to leave now. One, a rather large and ungainly girl of about fifteen years, openly propositioned both of us in Zeke's absence. I told her to wait by the dinghy that was ashore and the big hairy one would return soon. She was delighted and swam off awkwardly to await his arrival. I was frankly a bit suspicious about such an open invitation. I watched as Zeke approached the dinghy and she confronted him. He kept looking around to see if anybody was watching, and pulling her clutching hands off his body. He left her on the little beach near the church, a rejected figure. Now, Zeke had been amongst the natives much more than I. He knew more about their customs, and he turned her down, at least temporarily. I was laughing when he came aboard. He said it was not funny, that if you accepted the advances of a lady, you had to marry her! I asked the priest about that, and he said it wasn't law, but it was an unwritten rule among the people.

Zeke found an abandoned shack and took his gear ashore. *Sea Lion* was just too far away to commute by bus to his work. Now, that made sense to me.

The temptations were great; not all the young things were large and homely. There was one in particular. She would hang on the gunwale and look up smiling with the

wet T-shirt clinging to blossoming young breasts. She'd let go with one hand, roll over in the water to show me her lovely little bikini-clad bottom, then look into my face and smile fetchingly. This usually happened when fishermen were working the old stone trap not forty feet away. She never came alone and very seldom without witnesses at the stone trap. My reaction was to hand her Bri. The moment I made that commitment, all the other pretty young things stopped swimming out to *Sea Lion.* Only Loveliness with her homely young friend, and sometimes a brother, came to cavort in the water with Bri.

The fishermen working the stone fish trap seemed to approve of the way I was handling the situation and started leaving a few fat baby mackerel on the gunwale when they headed for home. The working of that trap was an ancient marvel. It was laid out in a wide V. I'd dived with mask and flippers to inspect it in their absence. It was truly old. At the apex a short, straight chute ended, where men could stand head and shoulders out of the water with a net in hand. The natural migration of young mackerel led right into the V. That bay between the outer reef and the mainland must have been nature's hatchery. The fish were about six inches long and very fat.

Lazy days floated by. Ripe fruit hung from the boom and lay within arm's reach about the sultan's bunk. Bri and I lounged on mattress and pillow. We rolled off into the clear warm water any time we wanted and went forward from under the awning for shampoos in warm squall raindrops.

Zeke came by for visits bringing news from the port, and Bri eagerly waited each day for her swimming companions.

One day my cut-off Levi's were missing. I searched the vessel, and dived in with mask and searched the whole

anchorage. There was no trace of the cut-offs. Worst of all, my last eighty dollars was in one of the pockets. I was stone-broke.

I had to go ashore and send a telegram back to the States for some money. Bri came with me in the dinghy, and we met Loveliness at the little beach landing by the church.

The suggestion was made that Bri stay at her house, and I walked with them. They lived in a regular frame house with a large yard front and back. Immediately I was treated as an in-law. I noticed that nothing hung on the walls. Each room had only the barest furniture called for. It was a large family, and most living radiated out from the kitchen. Bri called the mother "Mama," and that was that.

A bus ran into town, but I let it pass and walked. Life along the road was a strange mixture of midwest United States and South Sea Islands. It was very unlike the French islands. I saw a tree with ripe avocados in a yard. I knocked on the door and asked for one. The people were delighted and insisted I take several. Presently the priest came along the shaded road on his Honda. We discussed theft. It was his opinion that the native people were not thieves. I said that it was my observation that they would take anything left unguarded, even a pair of worn-out thongs. He maintained that the years of colonial rule simply had not been able to instill the concept of property rights. Some practiced it and some didn't.

As we parted, he invited me to come by his quarters. I regret that I never made it, for he was an unusual churchman.

Once in town, I sent a telegram to my old friend and business manager. I asked for money and news. I thought that perhaps there might be nearly a hundred dollars still on account. The way we were living didn't cost a lot of money, but being stone-broke is a disease.

I call it "brokitis." It makes one feel very low. It pervades every action, even the way one walks.

I went by the cutter. Zeke and the old man were at work. The old man was converting her to a refrigeration vessel to carry fish from distant islands. It seemed a waste to me; she was a classic. She had an offset reefing bowsprit and a gaff mast taller than most jib-headed rigs. There were a few examples of fine woodcarving left in what used to be her main salon. The "stick" was to be cut off and a big used diesel installed. The hull was deep and totally unsuited for reefs and shoal water, and it all added to my miserable state, but why knock an old man's dreams? He was an old salt and his work was proper. He was cussing Zeke's ineptness as I left.

On the way to *Sea Lion* I stopped at the hotel. The bar was still closed. It was a lonely walk back to Ngatangiia.

Bri was delighted with her new "family" and insisted on sleeping over. I didn't see her much for the next couple of days, and took to roaming the coconut island.

The island covered about three acres, and I dreamed. An acre could be cleared and mangoes planted among the coconut with a couple of varieties of banana and papaya. The climate was ideal for year-round crops of anything you wanted to plant. A wharf could be built for the sailing vessel, with a small barn and animals just ashore. A thatched-roof farmhouse with maybe even a windmill! Chickens in the yard and fresh fish all about. Too much for one mortal. With a bit of dredging, the whole place could be a self-supporting safe marina for all the vagabonds afloat! God, how my head spun!

Spin was about all it did.

A few questions answered by the fishermen tore my dreams asunder. The Cook Island government encouraged only those in the Cook Island government. Paradise was getting on my nerves.

After a week, wherein Bri's "family" seemed deter-

mined to make me a member, the answer to my telegram arrived. John had sent money from his own pocket; mine had been spent in union dues, etc. *Esquire* magazine might buy a story already written. The earthquake in L.A. wasn't so bad. (I didn't even know there had been one.) What was my next address?

The money from the telegram was paid in New Zealand dollars. Not wanting to spend any of it on a telegram, I sent John a letter telling him to send mail in care of the Port Director, Suva, Fiji.

In preparing to return to Avatiu Harbor to provision, I stowed the sultan's bunk and brought Bri aboard. The latter was not easy. She was a princess ashore and only the first mate aboard. We got to bed early.

We started at daylight, and it was a tricky business getting all those anchors aboard. Especially the big fisherman. I picked it up in the dinghy last. There was a light breeze from the north that gave me a beam wind on the port side at the pass. *Sea Lion* was skittering around in the variable current at the end of the small nylon line ashore. My mouth was dry from the effort of getting the anchors aboard, and the uncertainty of my ability to sail out of there. I threw the nylon line off the cleat and raised the main.

Much to my dismay, it had a reef tucked in! Too late. We were under way and I raised the headsails. *Sea Lion* caught the light airs in her reefed main and started for the pass. Waves outside were from the ordinarily prevailing easterly wind and crashed especially heavily on the reef to starboard. The moment *Sea Lion* was in the middle of the narrow pass, the wind faltered and she was practically at the mercy of the shifting, skittering current. My heart was in my throat! She was falling off the wind anyway, so I tried to jibe about. She answered, and a puff of wind came at the same time Bri was scrambling up the companionway ladder. We went on the reef! There

wasn't enough room to complete the turn, and she ran square up on the reef! Keel crunched coral, she floundered, and the sails flapped crazily.

Well, that was it, I figured through the tears. *Sea Lion* was done for and our journey ended.

The dinghy was tied up to the taffrail. We weren't sinking; in fact we were high and dry, lying over on the hard chine. I looked into the water and realized that if necessary I could take Bri and walk ashore. We were on the inside of the reef, and it broke the crashing waves before they reached *Sea Lion* with much force. Frantically, I set about trying to get an anchor out to deep water in the pass. I dumped the big fisherman into the dinghy, but the chain ran out and pulled it into the water as I tried desperately to row. Back aboard, I was horrified by the sound of her hull crunching the coral! I left the sails up to help quiet her wallowing roll. Bri wouldn't stay below, and scrambled about the mess on deck like a wee monkey.

Trying to catch my breath, I saw several canoes coming. Some of them were the fishermen from the trap. One had an outboard, but it didn't run. There was a hurried consultation, and they advised taking down the sails. I did so, and passed Bri to a woman in one of the canoes. Under the direction of one of the fishermen, we climbed the shrouds till our combined weight caused her to roll up on the chine, then we all let go, dropping back in knee-deep water. She would fall back on her keel and bounce a few inches toward deep water. Many times we repeated this maneuver, along with pushing and grunting on bow and stern when waves coming over the reef gave her momentary buoyancy. Finally she was afloat! I scrambled aboard the mess and ripped up the cabin sole expecting to see water gushing in. Not a drop! When we got the big fisherman anchor aboard, the shank was bent. The shank was drop-forged steel two inches through. In

the fracas *Sea Lion* had come down on the anchor with all her weight, the fluke stuck exactly in the middle of the keel at forefoot. Definitely a fluke!

One of the people in canoes was Tutai. While we all chattered and laughed in the anticlimax, I sent him back for that quarter-inch nylon line which was still secured to the coconut tree. Some of the men were standing there on the inside of the reef holding *Sea Lion* tethered, while I squared away the mess and shook that reef out of the main. Tutai returned with the line and wanted to help. The wind had become steady and fresh, still out of the north. I sent Tutai to the weather side of the reef with that quarter-inch line and instructions to snub her off if the wind failed. Bri was passed aboard and the full main raised. *Sea Lion* gained steerageway, and I ran up the headsails. Tutai said he would hold on to the line and climb aboard if the wind did not fail. He ran along the coral in knee-deep water as *Sea Lion* gained momentum. By the time she reached the pass, she was doing six knots and nobody could have held to a quarter-inch line! Tutai tried, but he was washed off the end immediately. It was my first experience singlehanding without an engine.

We sailed directly back to Avatiu Harbor. I anchored near the seawall that paralleled the main road. *Sea Lion* was Mediterranean-moored to the high concrete wall. No gangplank of suitable length was available. It was necessary to use the dinghy. I did not fancy going to sea without looking at her bottom dry. A local fishing boat was sitting up on barrels farther down the wall. It had been set there by the big dragline working around the harbor.

For a modest fee the operator started tracking that big machine while I scrounged up five oil drums and wood-scrap blocking. With slings made of heavy rope and wire, the dragline hoisted *Sea Lion* high and dry.

There was some rearranged lead along the keel.

Planks along the starboard chine were badly dented. Soft cedar had absorbed the pounding coral.

I wanted to do something for the fishermen who'd got her off the reef. A party. Pig cooked in the ground! Beer!

Bri's Ngatangiia "family" were delighted to have it at their house. *Sea Lion*'s grounding was a big event right then. Preparation began for ten fishermen and their families. Masses of taro, two pigs, oranges, coconut, and many cases of beer.

The morning of the party a large, square hole was dug in the back yard. A blazing fire consumed limbs and logs all morning. Large, smooth stones were put in glowing coals, and more fire piled on top. Starting with three men in the morning, that back yard began to fill up. Soon there were thirty or forty people.

About the middle of the morning I discovered that two of the fishermen would not be welcome. Some kind of family feud. I finally persuaded the father of the house to let them come. When I went to fetch them, they refused to attend. I gave them each ten dollars.

Women were busy in the kitchen preparing sweet-potato-looking taro. They peeled oranges to eat with fresh coconut chunks. Children ran and played through and around the house. The hot stones were dug out of the coals. The chunks of fresh pork were wrapped in banana leaves; each side dish was wrapped the same; then all was wrapped together in a ball with wet burlap and placed on the coals and covered with hot rocks and dirt.

By late afternoon the back yard was getting pretty drunk. Tutai showed up and was practically set upon. Because he was a "jailbird," they said. I had to talk to him in the front yard. I gave him ten dollars and advised him to catch a vessel out of Rarotonga. He wanted to go on *Sea Lion,* but understood he'd have to have a vessel to pay him as a hand.

The pit was broken open to release delicious aroma and succulent food. It was good, and there seemed to be plenty. Most of the men were full of beer. I couldn't fully enjoy it. Couldn't get my mind off the local status system. By dark some of the drunk men were making mean sounds to each other, so I collected Bri and caught a ride back to *Sea Lion*.

Marine supplies were not plentiful in Rarotonga. In the days that followed, Bri found herself a new "family" living near the harbor. I managed to locate some epoxy putty to fill in the dents. I also puttied in Vane Jane's little rudder to make it smooth. After I had sanded it all down, the patches were ready for bottom paint. There was a pint left over from the yard in Papeete. I discovered that fancy bottom paint had a major drawback; you couldn't take it out of the water!

Deterioration was noticeable daily. When the new paint dried, it was apparent that *Sea Lion* had to go into the water quickly. I wished I'd used common fisherman's red bottom paint.

The dragline's clutch slipped, setting *Sea Lion* back in the water none too gently.

It was time to provision for the passage to Suva, Fiji. Bri's new "mama" was good to her. She was a seamstress and made Bri a new cotton dress. It was so well made and simple Bri could button it herself. I asked the lady to make three more. It was the only way she'd let me pay her for taking care of Bri.

The aftermost panel forming the sultan's bunk was left in place. It made a seat at the tiller. Two orange crates fitted under it. One was filled with fresh local oranges, the other with fine-skinned purple avocado.

Sailing out of port is always a strange time. When you let go shore, all you need had better be aboard. Timing must mean something. Even a few hours can cause you to be in the wrong place days later. I had already cleared

port and waited only for a hunch. Just waiting for a
feeling. That feeling was to get away from life ashore
more than get to sea. Bri's health always deteriorated
ashore. The "mamas" were ever ready to hand out
candy, and bugs ate her.

Bri had acquired several new stuffed critters in Rarotonga. She knew something was up when I put them
aboard. She was determined not to sail. She pulled every
trick. After a temper fit she was sitting on her bunk looking very pitiful, and I said, "Look, kid, you're my good-
luck charm. If I leave you here, *Sea Lion* might sink." Her
expression changed to that solemn stare I call the "fish
eye," she put her thumb in her mouth, lay down on the
bunk with her back to me, and went to sleep. We would
sail in the morning.

Avatiu Harbor had been a dull and uninteresting place
until that morning. A vessel sailed in from New Zealand,
and just as I was heaving in the anchor, Henry on *Challenge* arrived. I would like to have visited, but the die was
cast.

# Chapter Ten

ON THE MORNING of May 12, *Sea Lion* cleared the outer reef of Avatiu Harbor. I had only one New Zealand twenty-dollar bill in my pocket. Bound for Fiji on a fine south wind.

I chose the southern route around the Tonga group. A mistake in the month of May, but I didn't know it then.

With Rarotonga a speck on the horizon astern, Bri lost her grip on the weather running backstay and went headfirst into the cockpit. One of the orange crates had worked out from under the seat, and her chin hit square on its corner. Her chin was cut wide open. I sat her on the lee bench seat, bathed the area with Merthiolate, applied an antibiotic ointment, and bandaged the cut tight. She didn't even cry. One piece of tape went over her chin and the ends stuck down on her neck, the other came under and up and stuck to her cheeks. She laughed in the mirror at the sight of the funny-looking bandage, then saw blood on the front of her new dress and cried as she went off to sleep . . . late for the daily nap she never took ashore.

That "sea feeling" returned with no land in sight. Fine weather and a good wind just forward of the beam. Ever notice how you can't think when you see what you're looking at? To me, that's the "sea feeling"—no past and no future. It's all *now* at sea.

Our course was just south of west, enough to clear the Tonga Islands, then we'd turn northwest for Suva with only the Minerva Reefs to contend with.

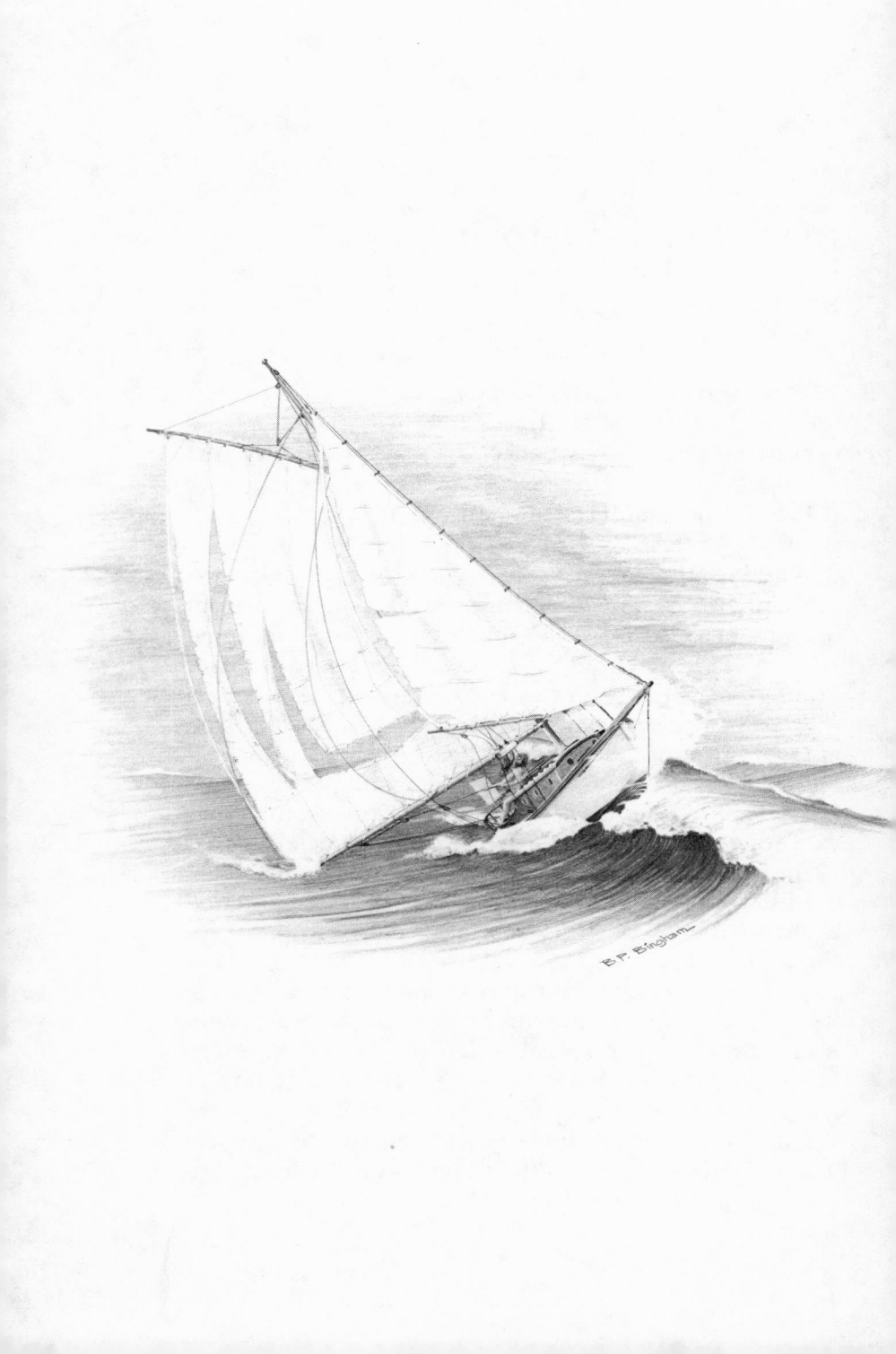

B.P. Bingham

I had bought two thick cast-aluminum cooking pots with lids back in Papeete. One, the large one, was for cooking soups, stews, and other one-dish meals. The small one was for baking bread only . . . sometimes popcorn. I baked on top of the stove. Beans were simmering and corn bread baking when Bri awoke feeling her chin. She went to the mirror in the head. She laughed. I've never seen such a brave person, young or old.

After supper I reefed the mainsail and read *Scuppers, the Sailor Dog* twice before sundown. I slept in the cockpit, so we both had a lee bunk.

At sunup the wind shifted to southeast and held steady. I shook the reef out and called Vane Jane to duty. Away we sailed with the wind on the quarter and no fear of jibes! What a delight that vane was.

For the first time I could not get time tics on the radio and missed taking a morning sight. After being informed of my great good luck back in the Tuamotu, I was determined to keep a close track of our position. All day I searched the dial for that comforting sound.

By suppertime the wind pulled east and freshened. The sky cast over, with long rollers from the south. Vane Jane was keeping her stern to it and holding a heading within ten degrees. After supper I tucked in a reef and a light cold rain started. The wind picked up. That cold rain kept me from sleeping in the cockpit, and shortly after we'd gone to bed, the wind had grown to a point where Jane couldn't hold it without shortening sail. I scandalized the main. Working naked in the rain and returning to warm, dry clothes was superior to foul-weather gear. The ship's bell was tied to the fishline, and its clanging woke me around midnight. By the time I got into the cockpit, it had stopped. Some very big fish had ripped the jig off. As though the fish were a signal, squalls appeared. I was

up the rest of that night helping Vane Jane with her watch.

The time tics came in clear before daylight, and after breakfast the sky cleared for a morning sight, but it clouded over by noon and I missed the latitude sight to cross it with. A good strong wind remained out of the east, and Jane held the big rollers nicely on the port quarter with a reefed mainsail. I got a little sleep that night.

Next morning the wind pulled northeast, and we came to take it on the starboard quarter. There was a morning sight but again no noon to cross it with.

By sundown on the seventeenth, five days out of Rarotonga, it was blowing hard out of the north-northeast. All three reefs in the main and headsails were shedding stitches.

We called Bri's chin bandage her "soup strainer," and it was getting pretty stained by five days of food that had missed her mouth. I removed the bandage for the first time after a late supper. The cut was healed. She was delighted with her own little tube of ointment. She could easily spend an hour at the mirror, standing on the toilet seat to apply ointment.

That night the wind increased to a point where Jane couldn't hold course with the full reefed main. I struck it and went back to sleep holding course under jib alone. A few hours later a change of motion woke me.

We were heading south-southeast with a Force 6 wind out of the northwest. By daylight I had full mainsail back up, and we were beating into a high, gusting west wind. Fouled log and another big sea creature carried away another jig. All that day we beat into a west wind. At sunset there were mackerel clouds, but the wind had eased some. I left sails sheeted in tight and tried to sleep in the weather bunk. It was hopeless. I took the companionway ladder out of its brackets, stowed it in the head, and went to sleep on the cabin sole, my head at the base

of the mast. I figured the wind would continue to fall in the night, and I desperately needed sleep. Some time later I was suddenly wakened by seawater pouring through the companionway onto my feet! Without the ladder, I had to go "salmon-like" up into the cockpit. *Sea Lion* was lying down! The wind had increased to gale force and the main was pressed almost into the sea. Green water was rushing over the coaming into the flooded cockpit and pouring into the cabin!

I dived for the mainsheet and threw it off, but one of Bri's stuffed dolls jammed the block . . . momentarily. When the dismembered doll cleared the block, *Sea Lion* stood back up, and I eased the headsail sheets. In a second, all the leeches were popped off the sails! God, it was dark and blowing, with the cockpit *full* of seawater! The small drains couldn't handle all that water, so I started bailing. By daylight the main was reefed and *Sea Lion* hove to. It was blowing a full gale!

It was also Bri's birthday. She was four years old. We fired up the stove and started baking a birthday cake. It was to be chocolate and fresh-grated coconut. It flew off the stove and landed upside down in the head. I started over. The next one landed on the cabin sole. I scraped it up, put it back on the stove. We celebrated with scrambled cake. Briewfn was delighted, and gobbled the sweet mess down. There's a song in the back of *Scuppers, the Sailor Dog*. I couldn't read music, but after "Happy Birthday" we sang the words to our own tune.

By noon the gale had abated and I got a latitude sight. 25°11'S. That afternoon was spent drying bedding and sewing leeches back on the sails. The wind fell, leaving high, unruly seas becalmed of wind by sundown. We were seven days out of Rarotonga and far enough south to head northwest for Suva. Those Minerva Reefs were somewhere up ahead, and I intended to leave them well to port.

All the next day we wallowed in high seas left by the

gale. Bedding was dry, but nothing could be done about the paper towels and toilet paper. I threw it over the side and broke out the bolt of blue terry cloth I'd bought in Papeete. It was forty-eight inches wide. With a knife I cut great towels off it for wipe-up rags to replace the destroyed paper towels I'd come to depend on so much. To replace my toilet paper, I cut two rags a foot square and tied one on each side of the taffrail with a long string so they'd drag in the water. For Bri's toilet paper, I cut little squares, but had to issue them to her one at a time because she'd play with them if I let her have more.

There was no barometer on board *Sea Lion.* My reasoning was that she could only do five knots anyway, so I'd just have to take whatever was coming, whether I knew it or not. By now I was wishing for *something* to tell me when to shorten sail!

By sundown the wind had increased to about Force 4, and we were really "marking it off." It was a good night's run, and I got some much needed sleep—the last such sleep for a long while.

Next day was bath day. The dishpan, a four-gallon clothes boiler I'd bought in Rarotonga, was set in the cockpit half full of cold fresh water. A smaller pot was brought to boil on the stove. The boiling water was poured into the dishpan to the right temperature, and I'd sit on the engine cover step (now the hold step), and use a saucepan to pour the water over me, lather up, then rinse off. Then it was Bri's turn. It was delicious.

Baths finished, the wind pulled to southeast and increased to Force 6. Bri's chin was completely healed and her insect bites were about gone. I had a new one on my left little finger. It itched like hell and I bit it. I reefed the main before dark and had to scandalize it and strike the staysail before morning. The seas were high, and it was a rough ride under short sail. For the following day's noon latitude sight I had to stand on the cabin top

with one leg and an arm hugging the mast to find anything like a true horizon in the sextant. 24°48'S. The
afternoon was spent sewing a leech back on the staysail.
Bri was delighted to have me trapped in the cabin so she
could get at me. Being in the cabin so long in daylight,
I noticed that the cockroaches were thick. They scurried
everywhere. At least they didn't bite! The bite on my
little finger was getting worse. It was infected now.

By dark another gale somewhere was sending high
seas in from the west to cross our own southeast rollers.
Still Vane Jane would hold the course so long as the
proper amount of sail was carried. I was up most of the
night doing that.

Next morning I got a sight and at noon crossed it. In
five more degrees of longitude we would be halfway
around the world from Greenwich, England. While I was
putting the sextant away, the wind did a quick shift to the
east, *Sea Lion* jibed, and the mainsail ripped from leech
to luff, right along the reef points! The boom thudded
down on the cabin top. When I got on deck, it spooked
me. I had never seen the boom lying across the cabin
with its tip dragging in the water! Also, the weather running backstay had been carried away. It took most of the
afternoon to get the main down and unlaced. When it
was stuffed into the cabin, there was barely room to cook
supper. We wallowed west under staysail and storm jib.

Another acquisition back in Papeete was a Petromax
lantern. It was pressurized on kerosene and primed by its
own built-in blowtorch. Though it hissed loudly, the
light was bright for sewing and watching the cockroaches
scurry. I fell asleep in the weather bunk with one foot
propped against the mast.

We had porridge for breakfast, and the rip was
mended in time to take the noon sight. 24°03'S. The
main was up and flying in time for lunch of kipper snacks,
crackers, and raw onion. It was one of Bri's favorite

times, sitting on the hatch cover, sometimes with just crackers and cheese between us. Wind remained out of the east and stiffened. Those seas were very high and crazy, but Vane Jane was doing a magnificent job.

We still had some west to make to be on Fiji's longitude, and were taking such a beating trying to make northwest I let her run off. By the time I decided to try northwest again to check a westerly current set, the wind came out of the northwest! The Minerva Reefs were somewhere ahead and to port . . . I hoped. We were beating into those crazy seas, the yankee jib was in the cabin wanting stitches, there was a painful knot on my little finger the size of a marble, and I needed sleep badly. Bri laughed and played with her dolls. I told her time and time again to keep the damn things out of the cockpit when she was through with them. She always left them.

Somehow I got a morning and noon sight. We had passed the Minerva Reefs in the night . . . to port. The wind pulled more to the north and had a distinctly "heavy" feel to it. We hove to. The vessel was a mess. Bedding was wet from a leaking cabin, and in spite of the pain, I had to sew sails in damp, stuffy confines while *Sea Lion* pitched on seas now building out of the north. At least we were clear of the reefs. Nothing but water between us and Suva, I thought.

By suppertime the yankee jib was patched and I had broken three more needles. We were still hove to into the north wind when I put the water on for spaghetti.

Suddenly the wind did a one-eighty and came hard out of the south! Within fifteen minutes it was a full gale. The seas went wild. Waves big as barns bashed head-on into each other. The sound was awesome. We hove to on the new heading, making leeway on course. I was standing at the stove when three wooden bowls were suddenly sucked out the companionway hatch . . . right past my face!

Bri curled up with her damp dolls and went to sleep on the lee bunk. I had to stay on watch to keep an eye on the jury-rigged running backstay, as well as the rest of *Sea Lion*'s much too light rigging. It gave me time to think, but there were no thoughts. Just a throbbing pain in that little finger.

The gale was blowing itself out around midnight, and I fell asleep at the base of the mast.

Before daylight I was called on deck by a change in motion. The mainsail was slatting back and forth. We were becalmed. Bright sun broke clear. After a batch of porridge, we put the bedding out to dry along with Bri's dwindling assortment of stuffed dolls. I got morning and noon sights. 178°40′W x 21°45′S.

By this stage of the voyage, the mate was totally entertaining herself. She had to. She was also learning not to crowd the captain too much when he had gone without sleep for a few days.

Sundown found the backstay mended, yankee jib in place, and a light wind out of the northeast. We ghosted along more or less on course well into the night before the wind freshened to about Force 5. *Sea Lion* was really sailing for the first time in days. We couldn't make much north, so I decided to gobble up west.

The sea was full of large plankton. We'd been sailing in a sea of plankton for a day. I could see the tiny life shapes sliding past the hull, some big as quarters. Every imaginable shape, including shell-less eggs with a variety of colored yolks! I fashioned a cone seine net from mosquito netting and a clothes hanger. It worked well, and I brought up a cupful after a short drag. I imagined the egg shapes with their multicolored yolks would be delicious sautéed in butter. Raw, the green-yolk ones were tasty, blue wasn't bad. I tasted a red one, and it felt as if 440 volts had hit my lips! The shock numbed my whole face. Once I was washing dishes and rinsing them one at a time over the side. A string of blue beads the size of

buckshot wrapped around my hand and wrist. The shock was so intense I dropped the plate into the sea. My hand and forearm were numb for hours.

We sailed in beautiful weather with a beam wind out of the northeast. The conditions lulled me. I broke out the last bottle of Papeete wine. I had bought an air mattress in Papeete too. With just a little air in it, just enough to barely support my weight, I put it on the lee cockpit bench seat. The sleeping bag on top of it and me inside. Two pillows to hold my head up while I watched Vane Jane working. I could look up and see the full mainsail broad off and pulling. In my fancy it appeared to be one blade of a giant windmill, frozen in strobe. The lee bow wave snored by and the wine gave me a floaty feeling. It was delightful. Bri was asleep below, and presently I noticed lightning flashing in the sky ahead and to port. I raised up on an elbow and looked over the cockpit coaming. Way off in the distance a cloud bank was pulsating with light. There were no bolts of lightning, just constant glowing pulsations. It was a spectacular show, but I soon tired of watching it grow. I dozed off to a very sound sleep.

Not much later I landed on the cockpit sole! There wasn't a breath of air, and the broad-off boom was thrashing from side to side, its sheet making the cockpit a dangerous place. Everything was lit up with an eerie pulsating light. My head was foggy. I grabbed up the bedding and took it below. Back in the glowing cockpit, I went to sheet in the main. Just as I took the turns off the cleat, we were hit suddenly by a ninety-knot wall of wind!

The sheet was snatched from my hands, rove through the blocks, and the mainsail exploded! Boom jaws shot up the mast and jammed against the gaff and shrouds! *Sea Lion* was knocked on her beam-ends and held there for awful moments as I watched the mainsail disintegrate!

I looked down and saw the sea flashing by, frothing through the lee taffrail! We were moving fast . . . on beam-ends! The bottom was her sail; we were on a "bottom reach"!

Presently it subsided enough to let her stand back up. The boom jaws slid back down the mast and the boom tip trailed in the water. The mainsail was a tattered rag.

The air mattress was gone. I scrambled below to check on Bri. She had been transferred to the starboard bunk, along with the bedding and practically everything else in the cabin. If she had been thrown there, she landed in a crawling position, on top of the whole mess, sound asleep.

The sky was red come morning. I discovered that the yankee jib had also exploded. I struck it and sent up the tiny storm jib.

Bri came crawling sleepy-eyed from the rags as I stuffed the mainsail down into the cabin to await needle and twine.

"Papa, what's this?"

"That's the mainsail."

"You better get it back up."

She was right. I had better. That marble on my left little finger was now the size of a golf ball. The slightest touch sent a lightning bolt to the base of my skull. I tried to ignore it, wished for procaine, hoped it would go away, burst, or something.

One blessing: we had plenty of sea room as she wallowed along reaching in a light northeast wind under staysail and storm jib. The giant jib came out of its bag once again. There was a foot-square hole in the clew where I'd gone for patching the main back in the Marquesas. I sent it up for a main with the luff stretched between the peak halyard and staysail traveler. It eased *Sea Lion*'s rolling some, and Vane Jane liked that. We were moving along quite well, but not able to make enough north.

By noon on the thirtieth we had gained only twenty minutes latitude in three days. For the next three days I sewed on the mainsail. The seams between each cloth were popped out, and there were chunks missing all along the leech. I broke many needles trying to force them through four layers of brittle Dacron. Down to three needles, I became more careful with the stitches.

One should never go to sea with petro-plastic sails, except those stowed in sail bags below for spares. Cotton does not crystallize in the sun, and it won't mildew while stretched on spars and stays driving the vessel. You can sew cotton and it will hold the stitch. Dacron won't, and you damn near can't!

Morning and noon sights confirmed that we were on the other side of the world, entering east longitude past the 180th meridian. When I told Bri, she wanted me to show her where it was in *Scuppers, the Sailor Dog.*

By the second day's sewing, I was running low on sail twine. There were carbuncles under both arms from the infected finger. We picked up a small tuna on the short jig and feasted on "face knockers" (patties) for supper. The mate was getting so careless about leaving her dolls in the cockpit it looked intentional. I badgered her constantly and she seemed to enjoy it.

At noon on June 1, it was apparent we were going to blow right past Fiji unless we got a south wind soon.

Just before midnight we got it! A gale out of the south. The single whip sheet parted on the jury-rigged main, and it wrapped itself so tight and wet around the mast I couldn't budge it. The staysail popped stitches off its snap hooks, and I had to strike it. That tiny storm jib was driving us at hull speed on a reach back to the east! Before daylight those seas out of the south were monstrous. I made a discovery about what to do in case of many emergencies. Nothing! Just hang on and do nothing. At first light the wind jumped without warning, and came a gale out of the east!

That easterly gale was taking the top third off those monstrous southern waves and shooting them like water cannon! From the cockpit I watched them blast past, first forward then aft; solid gushes of water big as freight trains!

Then I saw one coming right at us! It was a bit forward, but we were reaching fast, and I could see the collision course. It hit *Sea Lion* square amidships and knocked her on beam-ends! Except for myself the cockpit was swept clean. *Sea Lion* was dead in the water, and the next one filled the cockpit! The ship's bucket was gone. I waited for the third. Suddenly *Sea Lion* lifted on a mighty cross wave, tilted up gently on her side, and poured the water out of the cockpit! I just hung there to the weather taff-rail and watched with mouth open as the water flowed around my legs and over the lee coaming!

By then the east gale had waves of its own, and *Sea Lion* was flying north, reaching on the tiny storm jib. I opened the companionway hatch to see what must have happened to Bri. All bedding was piled on the lee bunk. On top of the pile was Bri, sucking her thumb, knee propped up and legs crossed, shaking her foot in nature's rhythm and grinning! She reached a hand out to me. I secured the hatch behind me and crawled up on the pile with her to sleep while she played with my ear.

When I awoke we were becalmed. I had no idea for how long. Bri was sitting on the ladder eating cheese and crackers. "Hi, Papa. Your finger stinks." In fact the whole cabin smelled musty from being closed up so long. I staggered out into the cockpit to check the log. It was fouled. I opened all the portlights and the forward hatch. *Sea Lion* was bobbing and pitching on the uneasy sea with nothing aloft to check the roll. The ends of all sheets and halyards were in the water like so much spaghetti. The teak deck had a scrubbed and bleached look. The stern lantern was gone, so was the ship's bell and fishline. "Papa, how about pancakes?"

After breakfast Bri said, "I can't find my dolls. Where are they?"

"Well, kid, like I told you. This time the sea got 'em."

"But I don't have anything to play with."

"Tough stuff."

With the bedding out to dry, I started sewing on the mainsail. That thing on my finger had five green heads. It was kind of numb now. I feared that if I lanced it before the main was patched, I might botch the job and not be able to finish sewing. As it was, I ran out of sail twine. For a few minutes it was panic time, then I remembered that fine Penn Senator reel with three hundred yards of fifty-pound test Dacron, and continued to sew.

We were now twenty-two days out of Rarotonga. If anybody was expecting us in Suva, we were late. The stores were in good shape, and we had water for another thirty days. The hull didn't leak, but with a heavy strain on the mast, the cabin did.

Once cloth is wet with seawater you're in trouble. When it's dry, you can shake the salt out of shirt or pants, but that doesn't work so well with bedding. The salt absorbs moisture out of the air.

I finished the main by dark and started on the yankee jib after supper of beans and corn bread. Thank God, the dishpan was below when the decks were swept clean. Bri washed dishes in the cockpit.

Daylight found us still becalmed, and I was thankful. I started whipping the snap hooks back on the staysail with fishline while Bri slept. It was June 3. I had worked out the morning and noon sights before a breeze came up out of the east. The sails, all patched, were up and drawing. I lanced the finger.

Cut it open with a razor blade. Like cutting gristle. No pain. Then jammed gauze down in the multi-headed core with a match stick sharpened like a screwdriver. I twisted the gauze in that gruesome thing and the pain started to return.

Bri looked on intently. "Damn, Papa, don't it hurt?"

I looked the other way and pulled on the gauze. There was a grisly ripping sound and consciousness faded. About two-thirds of the five heads came out with the gauze. The rest was picked out with tweezers. It was tough and fibrous, like scallop meat. I poured the crater full of Merthiolate and wrapped the whole hand in a bandage. Almost immediately the red lines running up my forearm disappeared. I discovered that when a body has become accustomed to enduring pain and it is suddenly removed, one gets high! We were set west of Suva, so what? The wind had already blown from all directions, surely it would turn favorable soon. The sails had a whimsical look; their leeches carried the lines of a comic-book villain's scars.

We beat all night into that light easterly wind. Noon and morning sights the following day put us a hundred and fifty miles west of Suva harbor with an increasing east wind. I baked a fine yeast bread and waited for the wind to change. It didn't.

By daylight the seas were big and that easterly gusting to fifty knots. Both the headsails blew out! To rags!

The yankee knotted itself around the jibstay, and I had to go out on the bowsprit to get it down. I sat astraddle the timber with knees jammed under its shrouds and toes hooked under the dolphin striker struggling to haul down rags wrapped tight and wet around the stay. Suddenly I was dunked to my chin in green water! I abandoned the effort wet-ratlike and moved inboard to strike the tattered staysail.

Visions of the dream vessel, *Libra,* came to mind. She would have no bowsprit.

With a lot of cooperation from *Sea Lion,* I got her hove to under mainsail alone. At noon there was no chance to find a horizon in those seas. I went below and started patching the staysail. As the east wind increased, *Sea Lion*'s hove-to motion under main alone became very jerky.

After supper I decided to try beating into it with the main. I'd set her on a tack and go below to the lee bunk. It was impossible to sleep. With each wave she was smashed dead in the water and shrouds popped at the chain plates right beside my head. Bri was in a nest on the cabin sole forward of the mast. There was no letup. I'd lie there and listen to those lee shrouds threaten to tear the chain plates out of the hull at each wave crest! Dreadful. The bedding was soggy wet, and cockroaches dropped off the overhead onto my face.

Bri couldn't sleep and started puttering about the cabin. She said, "Papa, you know what we need?"

"What?"

"We need a dry mama."

Suddenly there was a loud *rip* and *thud.* I scrambled on deck in darkness to find the mainsail ripped from leech to luff! The boom lay on the cabin top, its end trailing in the water.

With flashlight held between chin and shoulder, I got those rags down and the boom lashed to the taffrail. We were running off before it under bare pole.

On June 5, *Sea Lion*'s entry in the logbook was "Bound for Brisbane."

It seemed as though the wind had always blown from the east only. There could be no sailmakers in the New Hebrides, and Australia was too big to miss. Bound for Brisbane!

# Chapter Eleven

IT WASN'T PLAYTIME any more. We were into it now and I knew it. Australia was 1,800 miles away. *Sea Lion* wallowed away before the howling east wind with not a shred of sail aloft.

I was very tired. Just let her wallow along wherever the wind and sea wanted her to go. What a difference with the wind aft. It was almost quiet.

After a big batch of porridge with raisins and nuts, we both felt better. Bri was bored without a single doll and went to her afternoon nap without protest. I soon tired of that rolling motion and set about getting some sail up.

I cut the boltrope in the mainsail's luff. It had torn right along the first reef points, so I still had about three-fourths of the sail, ragged as it was. A three-part fall was salvaged out of the regular mainsheet. At first I was stumped as to how to secure the sheet to the corner of the sail. Then I remembered the supply of walnuts. I tied one in the corner so the lashing couldn't slip over it and secured the sheet fall.

With that loose-footed main back up, the rolling ceased and *Sea Lion* started to move. I set Vane Jane, but she didn't like the unbalanced rig. She wanted some headsail too. The giant jib came out of its bag again and went aloft on the staysail stay. To make the luff fit, I just lashed the proper snap hook to the turnbuckle. It was sheeted with the staysail sheet to the traveler on the cabin top. An ungainly-looking rig, but it worked. It bel-

# Sea Lion

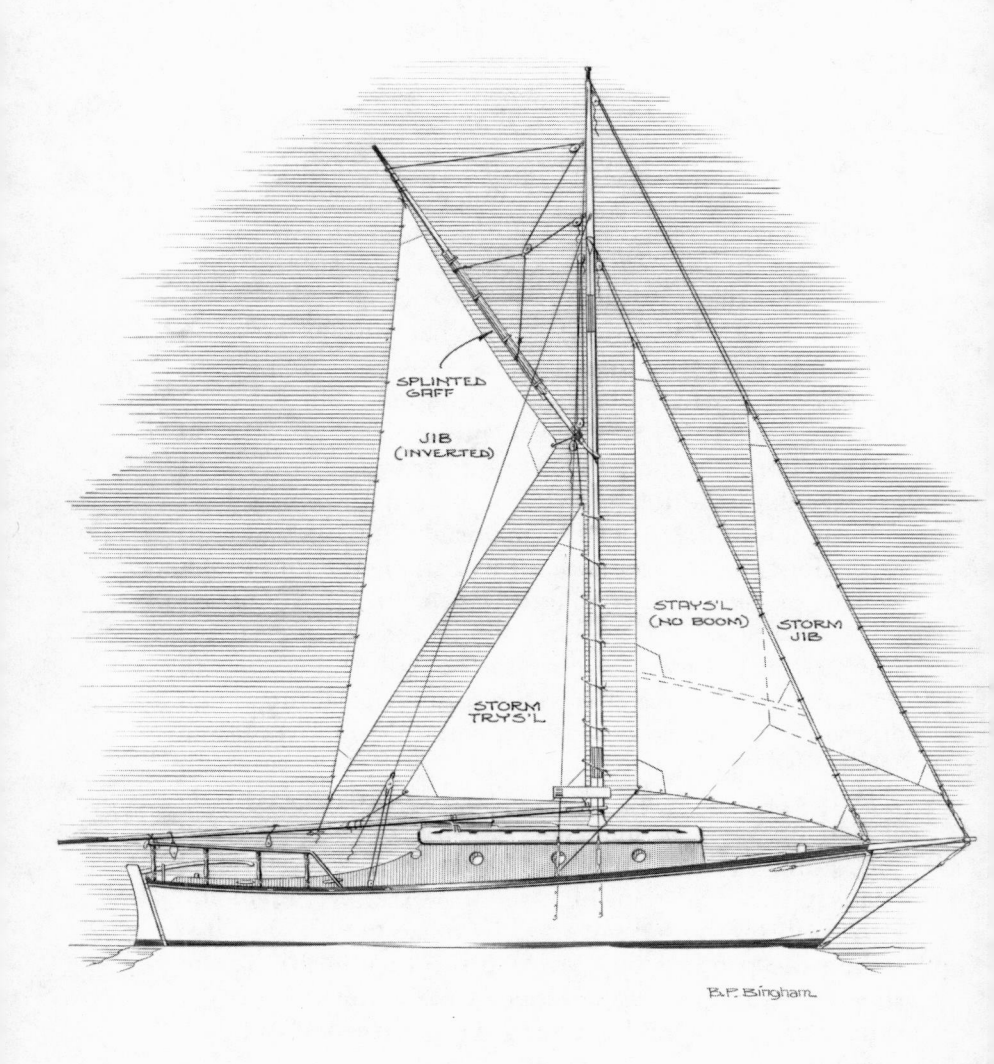

SPLINTED GAFF

JIB (INVERTED)

STAYS'L (NO BOOM)

STORM JIB

STORM TRYS'L

B.F. Bingham

*Rig upon arrival at Gladstone, Australia — June 30, 1971*

lied out at the bottom kind of spinnaker-like. With the tiny storm jib run up high on the jibstay, Jane approved. I discovered that if a downhaul were tied to the main's boltrope, it could be "reefed" by raising or lowering the whole sail. That device was also used to "fine-tune" the balance to Jane's liking. Once again *Sea Lion* was really marking it off! It was so quiet running downwind. Just the bow wave snoring by and the sea gurgling beneath her planks.

Before supper all bedding was drying, and we had cleaned up the battle mess of so many days' fighting into the wind and sea. The east-northeast wind held on the port quarter through the night and, though I slept soundly, I knew *Sea Lion* had easily covered her fifty miles from dark to dawn.

The next morning, that of June 6, sun broke clear over the horizon and agreed with the sea that we had done the right thing in heading for Brisbane. Through the whole day I didn't touch a sail or tiller. Just lolled about, read to Bri, watched Jane's magic, and puttered with cleaning and oiling tools. The taffrail log was stowed in its box. Some big creature had bitten the last spinner off and the bearing was jammed. It wasn't needed anyway; *Sea Lion* and I both knew exactly how fast she went under almost any condition . . . at least any we'd encountered yet.

*Sea Lion* was covering one degree of longitude and two of latitude each day. Her course was south-southwest and would remain so till we had cleared Conway Reef. Then we would make west.

One morning I noticed that Bri was very quiet below in the cabin. That usually meant trouble brewing. Perhaps she was after the sextant's mirror again! I lay down on the cabin top and looked over into the weather portlight. My view was upside down, but I could see her clearly sitting on the cabin sole. She had taken one of her wee T-shirts and stuffed a terry-cloth wipe-up towel into

it. She was pulling a head out through the neck opening. Then she pulled out two arms! Then she hugged it and breathed life into that creature. It actually seemed to have a personality. It had a very expressive face, depending on how she arranged the folds of smudged terry cloth and what light fell on it. They became inseparable pals.

175°40′E x 22°28′S at noon on June 8. Time to turn west for Brisbane, with nothing in the way for 1,210 miles.

Twenty-eight days out of Rarotonga and we hadn't seen even the lights of another vessel. Now we could expect them. We were entering the shipping lanes to the Indian Ocean.

It seemed miraculous. The wind followed us around as we made the turn below Conway Reef. We didn't turn due west, because I wanted to miss New Caledonia by at least a hundred miles. With a southwest course the wind came east-southeast. Every night I got a full night's sleep; during the day I lay about a lot watching the sea. It is always changing. Never the same for two heartbeats.

At daylight on the twelfth there came a big change. We were just about exactly a hundred miles due south of New Caledonia. Wind had been out of the southeast all night. Vane Jane was set in the eye of it. For the first cup of coffee it remained at Force 5. As I was pouring the second cup, the wind suddenly started cranking up. Direction didn't waver; it just started blowing harder . . . and harder. I sipped the coffee and watched. Instead of the sun rising in the east, there was a blue-gray eye rising from the southeast! *Sea Lion* was already passing hull speed. The seas were normal, with long, steady southeast rollers. Surely it would abate. It didn't. As though turned up by a rheostat, it continued to increase!

The jibstay was empty. Jane was having a hard time holding course, and I was about to haul down the main to its "reefed" position when it suddenly exploded!

The explosion was so terrific it broke the gaff jaws! The gaff was jammed between mast and starboard shrouds. Mainsail rags were jammed aloft in a great ball right against the gaff. There was no getting them down, and the wind began to scream!

I dashed below and secured the lee portlights. Bri had been wakened by the explosion of the main. "Kid, you stay below. I'll put out some food, but you stay below till I tell you to come out." I secured the companionway hatch and went to give Jane a hand at the tiller.

I couldn't know it then, but I was not to leave that tiller for ten full hours.

Jane couldn't hold it without me, and I couldn't have without her. I looked at the big jib sheet secured to the cleat atop the cabin not six feet away. Already I dared not try for it. The seas became very long—I mean it was a long way down the face of a wave, maybe a hundred yards . . . at first. There was plenty of light, but certainly no shadow. Already *Sea Lion* was surfing! She'd scream down the face of a wave, and it would take all my strength combined with Jane's "hydro-assist" to keep the vessel from coming up into the wind. The wind increased. I will try to describe it, though I know words will not.

In an hour or so the sea's surface started to separate in the blast of wind till one couldn't tell where water ended and air began, but you could taste it. It wasn't rain. The wind increased. It became a multi-chord howl! *Sea Lion* would catch the crest of a wave, now two hundred yards long, and scream away down its face. It was necessary to take the tiller at the fold of my lap, grab the weather taffrail with both hands, and pull with all my might and Jane's to keep her from broaching! I cursed the wreckage of sail aloft and prayed that the jib sheet would part.

Presently there came to be a pattern to the effort. First she'd scream down the face with the bow wave aft of my

position at the tiller. Toward the bottom of a wave there was a moment of great danger; she'd start to answer the helm and the tiller would have a heartbeat of mushiness. Let go the taffrail, shift position, grab the tiller in both hands, and shove it to leeward to prevent a jibe, which would also slow her enough to keep her from burying her nose and pitchpoling. She was then set up for the next one!

Soon I knew the wreckage aloft that I had cursed was a blessing! It prevented the hull from rolling. That screeching moan of the increasing wind became relative; we were screeching and moaning too!

Jane, bless her soul, thrilled to the work at hand. We would surely have perished without her.

To keep Bri from banging on the companionway hatch demanding to be let out, I cursed Boreas, the rigging, and the sea itself so she would know I was still aboard. I had gone quite mad, along with the elements.

To look into the eye of the wind was to risk permanent damage. I did it anyway. No matter how hard and tight I squinted my eyes, the lids would flutter like reeds against the eyeballs and I'd only get a glimpse of that swirling rifle-barrel eye of force before vision momentarily left me. Then I'd see the rooster-tail wake rising from under the keel twenty yards astern.

Time after time she'd scream down the face, falter at the bottom, adjust, and catch the next one. No longer did I want to let go the jib sheet. I protected the wreckage aloft against jibe. We had it down. This was the way to do it! Never mind that dragging warps crap! Let her fly, so long as you can keep her from rolling. That means sail aloft! And a long, straight keel!

After a few hours I was studying it in detail. Fatigue ate up the excitement and I became analytical. The keel was four inches wide. It had a good drag, that is, slanted aft in the water. That meant it was an inclined plane to the

water. You can't compress water, that's a law. As *Sea Lion* increased her speed, she was forced up on the inclined plane hydraulically, thereby reducing wetted surface and friction, thereby increasing speed, which increased hydraulic force on the inclined keel, which increased speed still further . . . till she fell over on the lee chine and tried to jibe. I know. I saw it.

It went on for hours. Thoughts of *Libra* came to mind. More beam. Perhaps some hog in the keel. Full bow with lots of lift. Cod head and mackerel tail. Dry quarters aft to steer from. Lots of sail. Storm sail aloft.

*Sea Lion* was traveling at a rate of speed to take breath away. Suddenly the giant jib shed all its snap hooks. Just like a zipper! The mass of sailcloth was suspended in that high wind between sheet and halyard. It began to whip violently—so violently I feared for the mast! I dived for the cleat atop the cabin. When I threw the sheet off, the whole sail pointed straight out from the masthead as though it were starched! So hard did the wind blow that the sail couldn't flop or flutter!

In another hour the ride was over. Jane could handle it alone. I opened the companionway hatch, and there at the bottom of the ladder was that terry-cloth critter squatting with one hand hooked in the drawer handle under the starboard bunk. He—it was surely a boy—grinned and welcomed me. It gave me quite a start. Bri threw herself at me and hugged hard. It was nearly dark, and I fell into a sound sleep. When I awoke, we were becalmed.

I lay in the bunk a moment listening to the gaff thud against the mast. I didn't even go on deck till I had a cup of coffee in hand. The giant jib hung limp in the water from its halyard. The gaff, with tatters of mainsail, hung swaying and bumping from its two halyards. She was a pitiful sight. With the giant jib aboard and down, we aired bedding.

The contrast between the sea now and a few hours ago was staggering.

The gaff came down easily, and I picked the rags off it. That break in the gaff jaws was mendable. Every muscle in my body ached, and both eyes were swollen black where eyelid had beat against eyeball.

I could still use the right eye on the sextant but would have been in trouble if I'd been left-handed. When I crossed the noon latitude sight with the morning one, I received a shock! I couldn't believe it and went through the numbers looking for the mistake. There was none. *Sea Lion* had covered two hundred and fifty miles in that day! Of course that is impossible for a twenty-five-foot waterline. I checked the sextant to see that it was in adjustment. Perhaps I couldn't see. The eye would be better by sundown, and I'd get Bri to bed early so I could work out a three-star fix. First I had to figure how to get some sail up in case the wind ever blew again.

That afternoon the gaff jaws were patched with resorcinol glue and tiny stainless through bolts. The biggest piece of sail aboard was the giant jib. I had to use it for a mainsail somehow.

I finished patching the poor old yankee and thought about the main. We had supper early, and I told Bri she'd have to be in her bunk and out of my way by sundown. She protested. I had pulled the guts out of her doll earlier to convert it to its original purpose. Although she had it reassembled, it was a damp critter and she hadn't forgiven me. "Now listen, Brief, I don't care if you go to sleep or not . . . but don't talk to me, you understand? While I'm taking the sight, don't say a word!" She grabbed up her doll and sat on the cabin sole facing forward with her back against the mast.

The three-star fix worked out to within ten miles of the morning and noon!

The following day, that of the fourteenth, we were still becalmed. The morning and noon sights of that day

confirmed that *Sea Lion* had covered a tremendous amount of ocean bottom. I know where we were when it started to blow. I stood at the tiller ten hours. It was blowing itself out when I crashed. Best I could figure, she was averaging twenty knots during most of that ten hours! I could believe it. Could anyone who wasn't there? Anyway, I cut ten miles off it for possible error and entered it in the log as Best Day's Run: 240 miles!

I felt we had the sea's "permission." A bit of wind came up from the west in the night and put us some south, still under bare pole. By daylight I had figured out what to do for a main.

The foot of the giant jib was stretched along the gaff. Not exactly the foot, but as much as would fit on the spar. The jib's luff became the main's leech, and it was sheeted by the peak! Upside down and soft luff, you might say. But it worked. The battered old yankee went back up on its stay and the storm jib on the staysail stay.

We were just ghosting along aimlessly with a light west-northwest wind. Now the boom was lashed where it had fallen. The jaws clung to the mast and it was lashed to the starboard corner of the taffrail. To fill in the empty triangle between that upside-down jib and the mast I used the storm trysail. A block was secured to the bottom of the gaff jaws for its halyard. That way it could be lowered by itself or with the main. The rig was strange-looking, but Jane thought it balanced quite well.

By noon on the sixteenth we had a fine southeast breeze and were romping away on course. Bri was still angry with me for disturbing her ragged terry-cloth doll. I promised to get her a pink teddy in Australia. Tensions eased somewhat.

Ever since I was quite young I'd wanted to go to Australia. It seemed like the last frontier. I had many images of what the place must be like. It would be a lot like paradise. Surely.

That night it rained hard, and about an hour before

daylight there was a loud cracking sound. *Sea Lion* shuddered. The gaff had broken in the middle! I waited for light to get it down.

We were in the Coral Sea now. We were also closer to the shipping lanes than I would like to have been.

The gaff had a nasty break, splitting both ways from the middle. I worked all day fashioning a scarf in the spar. The glue would have to wait for a sunny day. Maybe tomorrow. We wallowed along at about three knots through the night on the headsails.

Next morning it broke clear and I mixed up the glue. When the scarf was fitted together, I put three stainless steel hose clamps around it and drew them tight. By the time the glue had set and it was ready to go aloft, the wind died.

For the next day or so the wind shifted from all points. I noticed that it was possible to tack into the wind without a leading edge on the mainsail. It made me wonder about theory.

By the nineteenth we had a warm south wind and were riding easily west. What a treat to have a lee bunk! Next day the wind pulled southeast and freshened. Once again *Sea Lion* was "marking it off." That day from noon to noon we covered 135 miles, jury rig and all!

I was well rested and we were both in exceptionally good health. It was time to turn southwest for Brisbane. A place called Kelso Banks was just to the south of us. We changed course with a good east wind.

Morning broke bright and clear. While I was working the morning sight, the gaff parted again! The east wind held, but *Sea Lion* could make only half speed with the jury mainsail.

I scarfed the gaff again. It was getting shorter and weaker with each break. This time I used the two ash hoe handles that had been the "kid katcher" booms as splints to reinforce the spar. They were wired tightly to it. It was

finished by dark, but I waited for morning to put it up. We were in the shipping lanes from Asia to Australia.

The Pilot chart shows paths of past killer storms. The path is marked in red and gives the daily position of the eye of the storm and its date. Seems the Coral Sea is the borning place of many that go screaming off southeast headed for Cape Horn. The chart doesn't bother to record minor depressions, just the killers. Even a minor one would snuff out *Sea Lion*'s pitiful rig. I was already "gun shy," even before seeing those red lines.

Daylight came, and the wind was only about Force 1, so I put up the main, such as it was. We just ghosted along, and soon the wind died and the sky became overcast. I hadn't had a good fix for several days. Usually I welcomed being becalmed, but not here. I started baking bread to take my mind off the possibilities. The flour was full of weevils. I sifted out most of them, the rest would add protein. What the hell, they hadn't eaten anything but flour! While the bread baked, I fiddled with the radio. Brisbane came in clear on the AM band, and I found a music station from a place called Rockhampton. They were advertising a fresh-vegetable market.

I looked it up on the chart, and a thought occurred to me. With the radio out of its bracket and up in the cockpit, I sat astraddle the compass, tuned in Brisbane, and located its bearing by turning the radio around slowly to its strongest signal. I did the same for Rockhampton and marked its bearing on the chart. Where the two lines crossed was our position—approximately. *Sea Lion* now had RDF!

A radio direction finder that showed us to be sitting right square on one of those little red lines five or six hundred miles from Brisbane. By now I was so attuned to the elements that my ears would pop at the slightest pressure change. I could even tell from which direction a low came by the ear that was toward it!

All the rest of that day I just fiddled about nervously waiting for my ears to start popping. They didn't.

The next day we were still becalmed and the newfound RDF showed we were being set north by the strong current shown on the Pilot chart for this time of year. I thought about that vegetable market in Rockhampton. Who wants to fight a strong current in light airs? Besides, it was closer than Brisbane.

Presently a wee breeze came up out of the southeast. *Sea Lion* sailed along nicely for a while, making as much south as possible to compensate for the northwest set. Soon the breeze just played out. We spent the night becalmed again. I didn't sleep soundly. Bri said she wanted to "get going" so she could get that pink teddy bear so her rag doll would have some company. I agreed. Our food was running short, and we had no sure way to top up our dwindling water supply.

The next day we got some wind. It came straight from Brisbane. Even with her rags, *Sea Lion* could make an honest forty-five degrees to the wind in those particular seas. We continued to make west.

The following day, that of June 28, we got a fresh breeze out of the east-southeast. That settled it for me. I mean, if you're sailing with the sea's permission, better go where she wants you to. We altered course for Rockhampton. I could almost taste those fresh bell peppers they kept yakking about! The seas were flat and *Sea Lion* danced right along with the wind on her port quarter. Jane loved it!

The weather had a chill to it. We were no longer in the tropics. The sun was already as far north of the equator as it could go and had started moving back. It was winter down here.

To get to Rockhampton it was necessary to skirt the Capricorn Group, a cluster of reefs at the southern tip of the Great Barrier Reef. The chart showed a lightship

somewhere up ahead. With morning and noon sights the fix worked out to confirm those RDF positions of the previous days. I kept a close lookout for the lightship. There would be no sleep now—not for at least two days —so I ground some extra coffee beans and placed the honey handy.

I looked ahead once again and suddenly it was there! Breaksea Spit Lightship! Her light pattern confirmed it. Presently Sandy Cape Light was in range, off the port beam! I danced and sang. Bri didn't know why, but she joined in. Navigation worked! Forty-five days out of Rarotonga and we hadn't seen anything but wind, sea, rain, sky, and lightning till now!

Suddenly a very different reaction set in. We became quite still. There was land up ahead, and that's what sinks boats.

Night fell and it was cold. I fired up the Petromax lantern and it lit the cabin to bright sunlight. That thing poured off enough light to make me feel as if I was already in the city. It soon made the cabin a bit warm, so I took it out in the cockpit to replace the white light astern. Surely we could be seen from a great distance now. Bri, already stirred up by the singing and dancing, fluttered about the cockpit, mothlike.

Just before midnight Lady Elliot Island Light showed up off the starboard bow. Soon she slipped by two hundred yards off the beam. So long, Lady.

The following day Capricorn Group was sighted dead ahead. The islands were just on the horizon, and we passed them three-quarters of a mile off the starboard beam an hour later. *Sea Lion* was truly flying before a Force 5 southeast wind.

The chart I was using, the only one aboard, was of very large scale, and there was only one prominent navigation light left on it. Bustard Head. Beyond that showed a big island with the port of Gladstone behind it. I wondered

if Gladstone had a fresh-vegetable market. Anyway, it came before Rockhampton.

Suddenly there was another sailboat. Crossing our bow a half mile ahead! By this time I thought of ourselves as the only boat in the world. She was a jib-headed sloop about *Sea Lion*'s size. When her stern passed our beam, she was about a quarter mile off. There were five people aboard. I waved. Only one of them waved back. The rest just sat and stared.

Soon the Australian coast was stretched out along our port side. It was decidedly ugly. Mangrove swamps hid any shoreline, and there were low, round hills in the inland distance. They looked like purple gopher mounds.

Presently there was a big ship coming from where we were going. An ore carrier. It passed us a hundred yards to starboard. Night was falling . . . cold.

I fired up the Petromax. It was so cold that night I didn't take it out into the cockpit. I sat in the companion-way and drank coffee. Every once in a while I stuck my head out to look for shipping and Bustard Head Light. Soon the light was there. We passed it two miles off the port beam, and there were the lights of a ship coming up astern, aimed right for us and closing with frightening speed. I took the Petromax out in the cockpit. It saw our light and squirted by to starboard. We had a good Force 4 out of the southeast, but, damn, it was cold! I made a pot of hot chicken broth. Bri was bundled up asleep on the lee bunk. Her pillow was shared with the rag doll.

In a little while we were closing on the lights of the ship that had passed us. It seemed to be dead in the water. I cheated over close enough so that when we passed I could see it was not at anchor. I came about. If that thing was standing off and on, I damn sure was. It was a fairly large vessel and had extreme mobility. Our lights waltzed about out there in the chilling darkness all night. The Petromax hissed reassuringly. I'd sit at the

top of the ladder and sip coffee or soup until I nodded, then get up, take the tiller, come about, and turn it over to Vane Jane again.

At first crack of daylight the ship blew stacks. Black smoke billowed up. It had left colors up all night—German or Belgian, I couldn't quite make out. Then it sped away for harbor. We followed and noted its erratic course. Soon that was hopeless because the thing just ran off and hid in the distance.

By good light the water was a muddy red. The shore was about six miles off. It was obvious by the way we slid past the mangrove swamps that we were on a mighty inflowing current. I saw no navigation aids and could only guess at the course the ship had taken up behind an island.

Presently a fishing boat happened along. He was headed out to sea. I altered course so as to close with him. I waved both arms. The vessel didn't alter course or speed. I snatched the red flag off the "man overboard" pole and waved it at him. He still didn't alter course or speed. As his vessel puttered by our starboard bow not fifty yards off, he stood looking at us with a pipe in his mouth and one foot up on the gunwale, his arms crossed over his knee. Welcome to Australia.

There was nothing to do but continue on. We couldn't have done otherwise with ten knots of current and at least three from a following wind. *Sea Lion* flew silently with shore now on both sides. It was strangely quiet. The tiller felt mushy and *Sea Lion* would barely answer the helm, though the shoreline flew by.

It was about ten miles across the entrance between the island and mainland, almost a bay, but the freighter's erratic course indicated a changing and unmarked channel. Suddenly we struck bottom! It was just a bump, the keel slid on over, and we steered to port hoping that was the way to deeper water. Apparently it was.

Bri was delighted to see the shore. She pestered me

constantly about the hotel we were going to stay in. Presently we were sliding past massive port facilities on the mainland side. Six ore carriers were discharging their cargoes onto long conveyers running ashore. Up ahead I could see a town on a hill.

"Is that the hotel, Papa?"

With eyes sharp for a single mast we continued on. Presently up ahead there was an opening off the channel to port. A ferryboat came out and headed for that island across the way. Must be the harbor. Helm hard over, we headed for it. As we entered the side channel, it opened into the harbor, with a wharf pier to port and several small craft tied between utility poles in a row to starboard. I dropped the headsails. We had lost the wind except for cat's-paws coming over the wharf. There was an open space between two of the tall poles, and we headed for it. Inside the harbor the current was only about two knots. I dropped the main. *Sea Lion* put her nose in the space, and as the pole slid along the starboard gunwale, I grabbed it and secured a stern line. I payed out line, and the current carried her bow gently to the next pole. I went forward and secured the bowline. That was it; forty-nine days out of Rarotonga.

We had sailed across the Pacific Ocean.

# Chapter Twelve

A MAN CAME ROWING a skiff from the wharf. The channel was only thirty or so yards away, but an increasing current threatened to set him upstream. Much of his journey had been in climbing down the ladder to his boat. It was at least twenty feet from the street level to the water. The poles we were tied to were now sticking forty feet up from the water's surface. From the stains on pilings it was obvious the incoming tide had a long way to go.

The man was rowing straight for *Sea Lion*. He would be the first person we'd spoken to in forty-nine days. As he came alongside, Bri reached over the side and hauled up the wet rag tied to the taffrail. She swung it back and forth in front of the man's face and said, "Hi, this is Papa's shit rag."

He almost dropped his oars. I pushed Bri out of the way and asked what tide he expected. He allowed in a strong Aussie accent that it would be near sixteen feet and asked me not to go aboard his vessel, a big old powerboat, which was tied between the two poles upstream. Said he had new paint on deck and it hadn't set yet. I told him I hadn't intended to, and asked what the procedures were for clearing the port. He said we should stay aboard and wait for the doctor. He did not ask where we were from or how many days in passage. I asked him to please call the doctor and customs as he rowed away for the wharf. Bri, as though she hadn't heard a word of what was being said, demanded we go straight to the

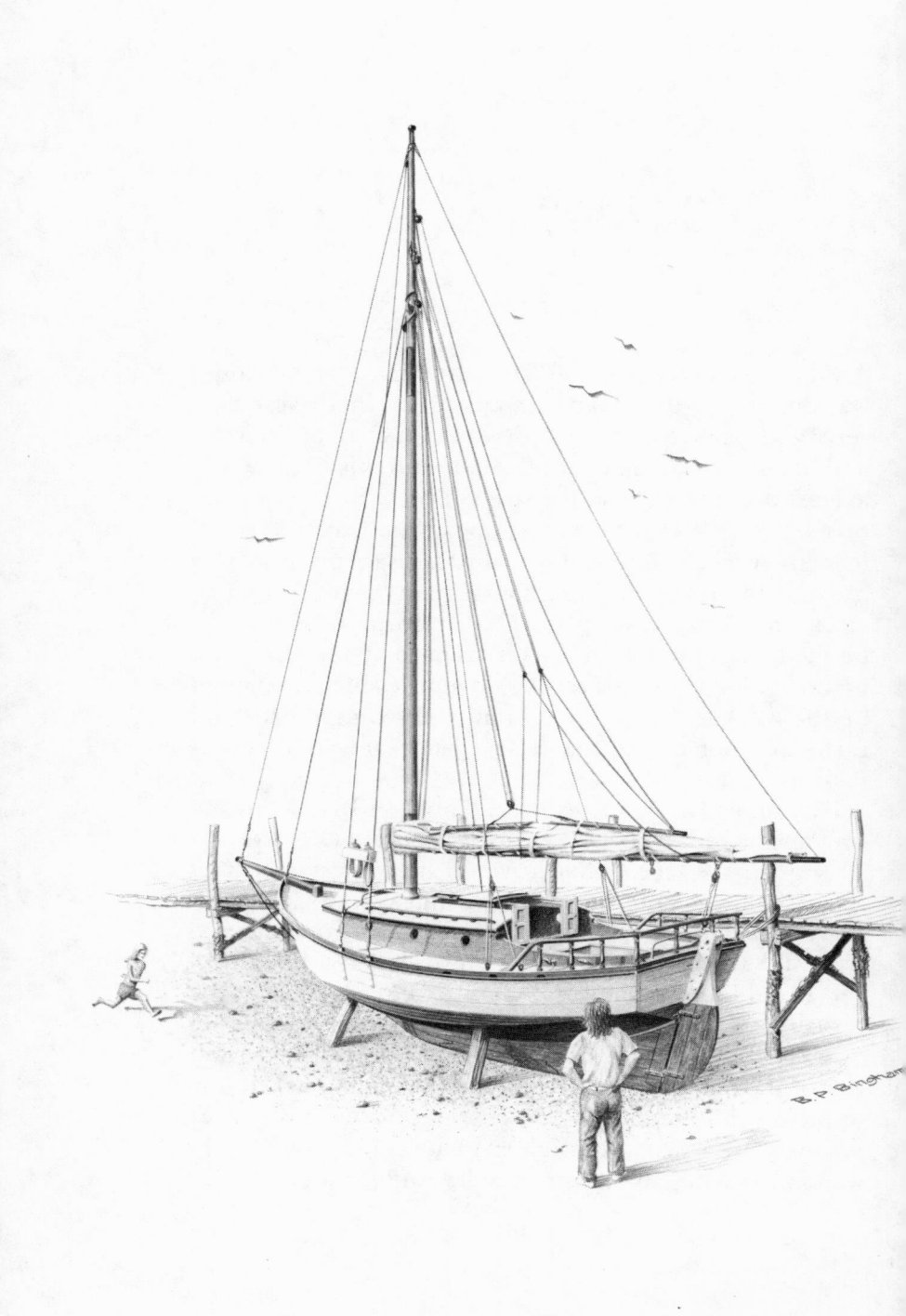

hotel. Right now. She kept at me while I went below to tidy the cabin up for the doctor. I didn't bother with trying to straighten out the ragged mess of sailcloth piled up on top; in fact, I felt it was a kind of badge.

As we waited for the proper authorities, I couldn't help marking the odors. Creosote, mud, and exhaust. Also the sounds of voices, machinery, and engines. It was alien after the sea. Yet I rejoiced in it all and felt like a teen-age sailor entering my first waterfront honky-tonk. I was as eager as the mate to be ashore. We looked longingly at the town up on the hill and waited for clearance.

Presently the customs boat departed from its own wharf and came alongside. It was official gray and had the appearance of a homemade PT boat. Two men, one civilian and the other uniformed, jumped aboard *Sea Lion* without asking permission.

I invited them below to the cabin and hoped the mate would keep quiet. Both the customs officer and the doctor acted as though everything was quite routine. They asked the normal questions and demanded the normal papers. Then the doctor asked to see Bri's smallpox vaccination scar. I asked him if the international certificate of vaccination card wasn't sufficient. No. He looked at the scar and said that I would have to have her re-vaccinated ashore! Her scar was tiny.

The homemade PT had been standing off in the stream and came alongside to take them away. We were cleared for port but under orders to get the vaccination first thing. We had an address.

As I inflated the rubber dinghy, Bri could think and talk only of that pink teddy bear that awaited her ashore. "Pump faster, Papa!" With the dinghy in the water I put together a flight bag of clean clothes, closed the cabin, and stuffed the New Zealand twenty-dollar bill in my pocket. The tide was almost in now, and I checked our mooring lines to see that the iron rings were free to slide

down with the falling tide. We would not be aboard that
night. As we rowed for the wharf, only four feet above
the water, I could see that the narrow channel we had
entered that morning was now a very wide marshy river
bay.

The wharf was busy. Ferryboats came and went with
the fishing craft. I tied the dinghy to a floating "camel"
that was secured to the wharf pilings. It was the main
camel, and many other vessels were tied to it.

Nobody paid us any particular attention as we climbed
the ladder and walked away toward the town on the hill.
The pier wharf had seen better days—along about World
War II, from the looks of it. There were very large,
unused asphalt parking lots with grass growing in the
cracks. We walked on. The mate kept her hand in mine.
It was strange to be walking so far in a straight line with
her. She chattered on about many things, and it all began
to come out in rhythm with our pace, pink teddy, pink
teddy, pink teddy . . .

As we started to climb the hill to the main part of town,
my legs trembled from the steady uphill pull. It didn't
bother the mate a bit. Presently we came to a sidewalk.
The storefronts became more dressed up as we approached the Grand Hotel. It sat at the main street corner exactly on top of the hill. We entered the lobby. Not
a soul was in sight.

As I banged patiently on the little bell sitting there on
the marble counter of the nineteen-thirties registry desk,
a man came out of the recesses chewing food.

"I'd like to make reservations for tonight."

"Yes, sir. Just fill this out. Where's the Missis?"

"It's the two of us."

"Very well."

"We want a bathtub."

"There's one to each floor." That meant there were
three to the building.

"Are meals served with the room?"

"Yes, of course, if you'd like, and we have some rooms with private showers if you'd prefer."

Bri said, "We want the bathtub!"

He showed us the room on the second floor and gave me the key. I left the grip of clean clothes in the room and we went to find the address for Bri's shot.

It was down the other side of the hill. I discovered it was the office of the doctor who'd ordered us to go there. He kept us waiting to boot! When he finally did give the mate her shot, he acted as though he'd never seen us before. His nurse was kind and made a big fuss over Bri.

It was late afternoon as we trudged back up the hill to the Grand Hotel. Immediately we prepared for the long-awaited bath. As the tub filled down the hall, the water was a faint rust red, but it was hot and there was no salt. We both climbed in and scrubbed and soaked and added hot water and soaked and played and splashed. It was delightful.

After we'd put on our clean clothes, and with our hair still a bit damp, we went down to the dining room for dinner. It was a great hall. Wainscoting and carved wood doorways. There were only five or six people for dinner in a room that could have seated sixty.

The meal was roast lamb with green peas, potatoes, cabbage, and mint jelly. It may not have been the very finest, but someone else had cooked it, and someone else would wash the dishes! It was delicious!

We retired immediately to our room. I was exhausted, and Bri needed only a pink teddy to complete her world. We crawled in between the clean, crisp sheets and soon were curled up fast asleep. No shoal water ahead, no freighters to run us down, no sail to be carried away in the night. Just clean white sheets to pass the night in.

We slept a good ten hours, and it must have been nine the next morning before we approached the counter to

check out. I reached in my back pocket and fished out the New Zealand twenty.

The man behind the counter presented the bill for some twelve dollars and I covered it with the crisp twenty. He started to laugh. I said, "What's the matter?" Whereupon he informed me that the twenty was no good! Was it counterfeit? No. What then? It seems that New Zealand does not honor its own currency if it comes from outside the country! I said he must be joking, and he called his bank to see if anything could be done. No. The twenty was worthless except in New Zealand, or perhaps the Cook Islands, where I had received it. Play money!

It was very embarrassing. I explained to him where we, and the money, had come from, that it was all we had, and where our vessel was moored. I asked him if he'd trust me for the bill until I got in touch with the States. Of course, sir; what else?

We made our way back to *Sea Lion* still without the pink teddy. Once aboard, I wrote letters back to the States and worked on the wording of a collect telegram to John.

*Sea Lion* had passed the night in comfort stretched out between the two poles. As I sat writing the telegram, cockroaches scurried across the paper. More scattered as I searched for small change.

The ferry came up the creek and moored to the wharf. Its crew was a young lady. I watched as she stepped ashore and secured the mooring line in a handy manner. The little harbor was a busy place for small craft. As I finished the letters, a large, fast motor launch came in smartly and tied alongside the ferry. Bri was pestering me to go ashore, and I wanted to have a closer look at the ferry's crew. We were about the middle of the creek in the dinghy when I noticed two men, one with an old Graflex camera. They were pointing toward *Sea Lion* and talking to the young lady.

We moored to the stern of the motor launch and were invited aboard by its skipper. He was a tall, stout, blond-headed young man who handled the vessel alone. Those two men were from the local newspaper. Since it was high tide now, they simply stepped aboard and walked across the ferry to interview us. Our pictures and the story would be in the morning paper.

In talking to the young skipper on the launch, I learned that there were no sailmakers in Gladstone. The nearest was Brisbane, some three hundred miles to the south. He was the superintendent for an island that belonged to a real-estate combine.

As we crossed the ferryboat to the wharf, I met the crew. Her name was Sally. She was a bit older than her movements had appeared from a distance. Perhaps thirty. She was lean and had a distinct frontier quality that I liked very much. She and Brief liked each other, and I knew right then we'd get to know this lady better.

It was late afternoon by the time we got to the top of the hill. I went in to mail the letters and discovered that all communications were in the post office—telegram, phone, and radiotelegraph. We were halfway around the world from L.A. I could call John collect just as he'd be getting into his office for tomorrow morning! We walked the streets of Gladstone and window-shopped till it was time to call.

The call so shocked John he almost forgot his good news. He thought we had perished at sea! *Esquire* magazine had bought the story and we had money on account! New sails! And a pink teddy!

I slept a lot better aboard that night. The money was there the next day. Bri got her pink teddy, and I started looking for the timber to make a new gaff spar. Seems Australia has plenty of hardwood and gum but no light softwood suitable for spars. There was something called Oregon pine. There was none available, but I could wait

for the next shipment. Two weeks. In the meantime, I had to do something about those roaches! I bought two cyanide gas "bombs." The instructions said to light them and run. Enough to do a two-story house! But I couldn't figure out how to do it. We would both have to be off the vessel for at least twelve hours, and she'd have to be unloaded of all foodstuff.

Our luck was running well in those days and held to the next. The young man who ran the island and skippered the launch invited us over to his place. Said he had an old wool pier we could tie to. The ferryboat captain agreed to tow *Sea Lion* over. When he came alongside, I noticed he was shorthanded. Sally wasn't aboard.

It was a long tow and a hairy one! That man threw the eye of a line over *Sea Lion*'s samson post and took off! I wanted to discuss the towing operation further, but the tiller demanded my presence. He had out about thirty feet of towline. Away on the ebb tide we flew! It was insane! The ferry was doing an honest eight knots. As we made the turn at the mouth of the creek, *Sea Lion* slewed wide and threatened to pull the ferry off course. He poured on the power, snatching *Sea Lion* back in his wake. With the added speed of that current the shore flew by! It was frightening. What if he decided to stop . . . or even slow! I let go the tiller and went forward to the samson post. I hollered for attention. He wore a hearing aid. He looked back at me and grinned.

I wanted to cut the line, but I'd never get back in the creek against that current. I started shortening the towline. It was hard work, but soon the bowsprit was over the ferry's transom and the dolphin striker chain was chafing his rub rail. He looked back again but didn't grin this time. The ferry was already going full bore and he kept it that way. The ore ships and piers slid by the starboard side at an alarming rate, and soon we were out to the wide part of the harbor entrance.

Suddenly the ferry veered away on a new course toward the island side. It soon became apparent that there
were several islands. We tore along on this new course
for another hour. We were headed for the boonies!
There was less and less sign of habitation. In time a high
wharf loomed up ahead. It looked more like scaffolding.
The shoreline pinched in on both sides and the ferry
slowed. There was a great wall of new earth just past the
scaffold wharf. It looked like an earth dam. The whole
place looked as though it had recently been gouged out
by reckless children. There was barely room to turn the
ferry around in the muddy water. The young ramrod
who'd invited us out to this place stood on a small camel
that rode up and down the tall scaffolding. He threw me
a line and I cast off the ferry, which churned up clouds
of red mud and flew away out the narrow inlet.

The power launch was tied to the camel, and there
wasn't room left to tie *Sea Lion* except alongside it. Once
secured to the launch, Bri and I joined the ramrod and
climbed a slimy ladder to the top of the scaffold. A gangplank structure went ashore from there. I commented on
the wild ride. He said it was necessary, for in a few minutes the water in the inlet would be too low to float the
ferry. The tide was over seventeen feet!

We got in an old pickup truck and rode the couple of
miles to the house, which he told us was an old sheep
ranch headquarters. On the way he had pointed out a
battered shed-like barn and said the pier I was to use for
debugging *Sea Lion* ran out from it.

After we had met his wife and kids, he offered a stiff
drink of the local Bundaberg rum. It was very effective.
I asked to see the wool pier. He pointed out how to get
down there, and I walked down alone.

The place hadn't seen a sheep in a long time. The
narrow pier ran a great distance out from the shed. The
pilings were local tea tree. Many boards were broken or

missing. There was now a smooth sand beach that sloped gently all the way to the end of the pier before it reached water. I could see the scaffold wharf sticking up in fading light about a mile down the shore. There didn't seem to be any sunset or sunrise in this part of the world. It just got light slowly, then at evening slowly got dark. It all had a lonesome ghost quality. Perhaps it was the ghosts of all those sheep that must have fallen off the narrow pier trying to load in time to beat the tide.

The lady of the house seemed ill at ease with her lot even before we arrived. There was a meal, and afterwards I walked back to *Sea Lion,* leaving Bri and her new teddy to spend the night at the house. I noticed she didn't call the lady "Mama."

When I got back down the slimy ladder to the camel, it was sitting on mud and the launch was heeled over against its mooring lines. *Sea Lion* was barely afloat, but the tide had turned and was coming in fast. I went to sleep feeling very uneasy about the situation and surroundings I'd got us into.

I awoke very early, and the tide had just turned. The camel, launch, and *Sea Lion* were now near the top of that high scaffold! As I drank the first cup of coffee, daylight started coming. I could see the wool pier was only about a foot out of the water. The earth wall in back of the tiny harbor began to turn red with the coming light, and I decided to go have a look at it.

♦ It was necessary to cross a deep trench at the toe of the dam. As I climbed its steep face at an angle, I had to cross deep erosion cuts every few feet. When I reached the top and looked over the other side, my heart jumped into my throat! It was a lake! Perhaps twenty acres of water! I looked down at *Sea Lion* tied to the spindly scaffold. If that childish dam I was standing on should break, there wouldn't be anything left below. Even with *Sea Lion* tied to the wool pier a mile away, she would still be in jeopardy!

I was wondering why my host hadn't told me any of the drawbacks in coming to this place when he came walking down the dam. Apparently he saw no jeopardy, and praised the beautiful view! I asked him about the deep trench cut along the foot of the dam. He said it was where some engineers were testing.

"Testing for what?"

"To see if the bloody crooks who built it put the proper clay in the core."

"What did they find out?"

"Nothing. There ain't even a bloody core."

"Let's get down off here while we finish this talk."

He followed. "It's all right, mate. The boss is gonna sue those crooks, and the engineers say the dam will hold anyway!"

As we went down the face and headed for the scaffold, he went on to tell me how the boss had impounded the construction outfit's equipment and how he himself had got in a gunfight with them when they came with a barge in the night to take it back.

I didn't see any earth-moving equipment. Under close questioning, it turned out four of them had jumped him and taken his rifle away. They threw it in the sea and left with their equipment.

Once on the camel, I asked if he had a tide chart. There was a fresh one aboard the launch. Flood tide for the month was in two days. I asked him to tow *Sea Lion* out of there immediately and I'd anchor off the wool pier till then.

"Couldn't do that now, mate, the boss is coming in from Brisbane today. Give a hand and shift your vessel to the camel. I'm off to pick him up right now." As soon as the launch was free, he fired the engines and, without warming them, sent rooster tails up as he roared away out of the tiny harbor. I watched him go and vowed to put some giant oars aboard *Sea Lion.*

For two days, every time I looked over at the earth dam

it appeared to be bulging near the base, and those seepage spots seemed bigger and wetter.

The lady couldn't handle Bri at the house, so she had been staying aboard and that made the dam seem even weaker.

The boss arrived and he was Australia's version of a big-time operator. Bri and I were invited over to his house on the other side of the island for dinner the night after he arrived. A middle-aged man who appeared to be his buddy, but was actually a manservant, drove us over in a new Land Rover. He also cooked the meal. The house sat on a hill overlooking the open sea. It was a beautiful spot, but the tacky new house belonged in a suburban development, and in fact the plans had come from one of his developments.

As the meal was being prepared, the boss pretended to be helping, and told me of his plans to turn this little sheep island into a resort community. It quickly became apparent he wanted to hear nothing but praise, so I quietly slipped off to the living room. There I found a stack of the last year's news magazines from the States! It was the first news I'd had of what had been happening. I became totally absorbed in the old news and let the two of them scold and chase Bri out of various mischievous operations. That news seemed good. At least there was no full-blown civil war as I had expected!

By the time the meal was finished, that boss was mighty glad to see us climb in the Land Rover and roll away from his paradise.

The flood tide finally came, and *Sea Lion* was pulled up along the wool pier till her keel touched bottom. I secured her there, knowing it would be a full month before she would float again . . . unless that dam broke. I climbed the shrouds and secured two lines to the masthead. The ends went ashore to guy her off in case the wind blew. As the tide went out, she bumped gently on the sand bottom and came to rest with her gunwale ex-

actly even with the pier. The angle of her straight keel exactly matched the slope of beach, so she was also level with the world.

The next day Bri and I started unloading the vessel. Great care was taken to see that no cockroaches were transferred to the pier. By late afternoon everything except hardware was stacked in piles up and down the pier for twenty yards.

The mate was to sleep up at the house and I in the sheep shed. Cyanide bombs were placed in forepeak and under the companionway ladder. That great awning tarp wrapped the entire cockpit, and all portlights and hatches were secured. I lit the bombs and closed the companionway behind me.

All the next day Bri played and romped up and down the beach. It was winter down there, being July, but less than twenty-five degrees south latitude. Only the nights were really cold.

I left *Sea Lion* sealed up for another night, and on the following morning opened her up. There was a carpet of cockroach carcasses on every flat surface! With a whisk broom I swept them up by the bucketful! Then I started on the bilge. It seems that the female roach drops an egg in her death throes. There were at least as many eggs as bodies. I built a small fire where the tide would claim it and burned them. Then every surface had to be washed down. A deathly sweet-smelling film of gray-green was everywhere. She was certainly debugged. The mate and I reloaded our vessel, making sure again that no insects of any kind were transferred. Soon *Sea Lion* was tidy and ready to move aboard, but there were many days to wait before the next flood tide.

One day we went to Gladstone with our host on the launch. It was a very limber vessel. Two big gasoline V-8s and very light construction. He drove it like a cowboy. He had supplies to get and we needed a mail call.

There was a good bundle of mail. The Oregon pine

shipment was still not in. We walked around town and bought knickknacks until I found the pub. It was the only one in town and brand-new. In a hotel it was. There was a separate place where Bri was allowed, the place where unescorted ladies and families could drink. It was not a comfortable place to have a beer, but I was feeling all right as we walked back down the hill to the creek.

We arrived well ahead of our host and found the ferryboat in. Sally was aboard, so we had a long chat. The more we talked and I observed her relationship with Bri, the more I liked her. She seemed tough enough to handle anything, yet was built like a dancer. I noticed that the people around the wharf respected her, and no one gave her a hard time about anything. I also had a chance to talk to the ferry's skipper, the one who had towed us out. He was about sixty years old. He had a strange attitude, and I discovered later that he considered Sally to be his girl. Actually he was a jazz guitarist. He owned a small island which he'd bought for next to nothing when everybody thought the Japanese army would be the next tenants. It was his knowledge of local waters that made him skipper of the mail ferry. In spite of his distant attitude toward me, I liked him. They all called him Lou.

Presently our host returned and we loaded supplies. In spite of being so spread out, Gladstone was really a small town. Everybody knew everybody else and the customs officers knew everything that went on. Sally waved from the wharf as we departed.

Back on the sheep island, Bri and I were sleeping aboard and having a pretty easy time of life. Somehow she didn't fret to go play with the two children up at the house. She didn't really like the lady, and when the lady refused to let us use her washing machine, I knew the lady didn't really like us. Soon the lady fell ill and left the island. I think she went to a hospital; anyway, she left the two kids with our host, a young man ill prepared for such a chore.

It wasn't long before he was in the launch headed for the mainland to find someone to come out and give him a hand. Guess who he brought back? Sally!

Sally was a very outspoken lady and quickly told me she was there to take care of our host's children, not me or mine. I told her if she needed any help to call on us. She did come to see us down at the wool pier every chance she got. She even let us use the washing machine.

*By this time the boss had come and gone a couple of times, but we never saw him. By the young man's attitude it was evident he wanted us off the island worse than we wanted to go, if that's possible. But he was a good old boy, and making the best of it, since nature was the judge of when we'd leave. One day he returned with the launch, and its bow was all stove in. That wasn't too surprising in light of the way he handled the vessel; what was surprising was that there were no tools, materials, or know-how on the island—except aboard *Sea Lion.*

The boss and his man were present at the time, and I told the man that I would repair the damage for a wage and reimbursement for the materials I used. He was eager to accept. It took several days—days working right at the foot of that Mickey Mouse dam. There was an old table in the sheep shed with quarter-sawn oak plank in its top about the thickness of that vessel's hull. I removed the damaged plank and dry rot back far enough to hold fastenings, then shaped and fitted the planks from the table. The bronze wood screws, bolts, seam compound, and paint were from *Sea Lion*'s stock. While I was working on it, the boss wanted to go to the mainland and was upset at me! Soon it was finished, and a handy job too. Everybody was a little nicer to us, but only a little.

The one bright light in those days waiting for that high tide was Sally. Although she could flare up like a gamecock if anything crossed her notion of what was right, mostly she was cheerful, and I liked that crazy twinkle in her eye. One night when the men were all over at the

boss's house getting drunk on Bundaberg rum, she put Bri to sleep with the kids up at the house and we spent the evening alone.

I told her we needed a "sea lady." I asked her to sail with us for Brisbane, and after new sails were fitted, if she liked, to sail on. She didn't give me an answer right then.

The day of high tide came, and I spent it straining mosquito larvae out of the big tank that caught rainwater off the sheep shed roof. By dark the tanks were topped up and the guy lines from the masthead were aboard. Our host—I call the young man our host because he'd invited us out in the first place—Briewfn, Sally, and I were sitting having a spot of rum up at the house waiting for the tide that would be in by ten o'clock that night. We had downed several of the silky drinks and the two other kids were asleep when the boss arrived. Now, to my knowledge, he had never been near the old house. It was a surprise. He sat and had a drink, pretending to be friendly. That was just the sort of thing that would send Sally off. I watched her eyes narrow as the boss went on with small talk. Soon his man came in and, by a very obvious schoolboy eye signal, let the boss know that *something* hadn't happened yet. Then he sat down and accepted a drink of rum too. It was obvious they intended to make sure we departed at high tide.

Suddenly Sally exploded! She tied into the two of them! She called them every name in the book and accused them of everything I had felt from the beginning. The boss's man slipped out during the tirade and she added our host to the abuse! I sat with mouth open and watched as she took them apart. The boss tried to make a comeback, but she had the goods on him. Our host tried to get rough, and she snatched up a butcher knife. About that time the boss's man came back in and gave the boss a "yes" signal.

He turned to me and told me our vessel was afloat and

to get off the island. Our host said to take Sally too! That wasn't easy, but Bri and I managed to get her calmed down enough to pick our way in darkness down to the wool pier. Sure enough, *Sea Lion* was afloat and pulling at her mooring lines to the pier. We got aboard and cast off.

I raised *Sea Lion*'s rags in light airs to the sound of our host, standing at the end of the pier, telling us he wished it hadn't happened this way, telling Sally he'd pick her up in town tomorrow, but not saying it loud enough for the boss to hear up at the house. Those rags caught the air and we made as much distance as we could on the slack tide—maybe five miles—then dropped the anchor. That ferocious tide was running out then at about seven knots! Bri was already asleep. Sally laughed and giggled at what she had done. We were both a bit drunk on the rum and fell asleep.

Before daylight *Sea Lion* was bumping the bottom and it woke me. I made coffee, and when the tide turned we pulled anchor, raised rags, and continued on in toward Gladstone. Sally woke and told me over coffee she had made up her mind to sail down to Brisbane with us. Brisbane was her home. Her parents lived there. She said we could anchor off Lou's island and outfit from the ferryboat. That sounded great to me. I didn't want to put *Sea Lion* back up that creek with her rags if I could help it.

Sally had good knowledge of the local waters, and soon we were anchored off a small island. I rowed Bri and Sally ashore and went back to stay aboard *Sea Lion*. I didn't trust that awesome tide, and knew nothing of the holding qualities of the bottom here. Presently the ferry approached and tied to the small landing on the island. A young lady tied the vessel up while Lou got out, keeping an eye on *Sea Lion*. I waved. He waved back, and they went on to the one house—his, I supposed.

In a little while I saw the bow of that homemade PT boat nosing out from behind an island in the distance. Once they were in view, they came at flank speed toward us. They came alongside, and I recognized the young officers from Gladstone. They asked what I was doing there, and I told them.

"You mean to say Sally's sailing down to Brisbane with you?" the senior officer asked.

"That's right. Why?"

They all laughed. "Better watch your step, mate. She's a crazy one. By the by, you have mail at the P.O." They put the patrol boat in gear and roared away toward Gladstone harbor.

I made myself some lunch of sardines and onion. Soon Lou came back to the ferry alone. He untied the lines, got aboard, and waved as he left, headed away from Gladstone. Having been up late the night before and consumed too much rum, I lay down in the cockpit for a nap. I slept soundly till I heard water slapping right next to my face! I opened my eyes, and *Sea Lion* was heeled over about thirty degrees! The water was gone! A few moments later she was lying on her chine in a sea of mud. It was at least a quarter mile to any water! That was startling at first, but I soon realized the mud was soft. I curled back up on the lee seat and went back to sleep. Water slapping very close to my face woke me again. This time I thought I heard voices in the distance. *Sea Lion* was stuck in the mud, and water of the incoming tide had reached the cockpit coaming before her buoyancy was great enough to break the suction of mud on her bottom. Suddenly she popped upright, and I saw Sally and Bri waving from the landing.

I got in the dinghy and rowed ashore. It was almost dark. By the time I secured the dinghy to the landing it was dark. Sally was different than I'd yet seen her. She was more relaxed and feminine. As we walked the long

pathway to the house, she told me they had had a nap too. Bri had stories to tell, when suddenly an animal came loping out of the bushes! I jumped back. "What the hell is that?!"

Bri said, "That's a wallaby, silly."

It looked like a small kangaroo. I didn't trust the damn thing. That long-legged rat followed us all the way to the house. Inside I met the other young lady; she was Sally's sister. Dinner was on the stove.

In the next few hours I was filled in on their lives for the past ten years. Sally lived there, and when the harbor was being built, she had danced to Lou's guitar for the construction workers. Lou furnished booze and music, Sally danced and turned them on. The island was a honky-tonk. Illegal, but not harassed by authorities, who knew construction workers need more excitement than the government pub provided. They had workéd this little gold mine for some years, but now the vein was petering out. There were no more construction workers. Sally and her sister were both quick to point out that there had been only dancing. Lou had taken to running the ferry to hold the operation together in hopes of another boom soon, but neither Sally nor her sister thought one was coming. They both liked Lou and stayed on to see he was looked after. They showed me his guitar. It was a fine old Gibson with an extra bass string built on. It occupied a place in the house like a shrine. I didn't dare pick it up or even touch it.

Lou arrived by dinnertime and after eating gave Bri and me the show. Sally danced and her sister served drinks. It was something to behold. Lou was a fantastic jazz guitarist with an incredible repertoire! The bass string beat rhythm as Sally bumped and ground. Bri was delighted.

I asked Lou what they did with all those worked-up, drunken roughnecks after the show.

"Oh, they went out on the island and beat hell out of each other. We never allowed fighting in the house."

Sally walked me back to the dinghy. As I was untying the painter, she said, "You know, there was never anything serious between Lou and me."

The next day Lou came by in the ferry to take me to Gladstone for final outfitting. He was sour and didn't talk much. I didn't blame him. I was leaving town with his talent.

I had been provisioning *Sea Lion* all along, so there were only details to buy. Like Bundaberg rum. The mail had to be picked up and a forwarding notice left. The port had to be cleared. In the big bundle of mail was a bill for fifteen dollars from the doctor who had given Bri that unnecessary shot. I went by the customs vessel and asked if they had any charts to spare for the coast down to Brisbane. They were very helpful and gave me three or four that covered the waters from Sandy Cape to the approaches of the Brisbane River.

When we got back to Lou's island, *Sea Lion* was high and dry on the mud bank. Seeing her like that made me uneasy, but she was in no danger and in plain view from the house. Bri had been having a great time with the two ladies and was full of stories about the wallaby, and an old cockatoo that lived on the island.

There was a big meal that night, and we planned to leave for Brisbane on tomorrow's outgoing tide. The tides of that area pushed millions of acre-feet of water back up into every creek and mangrove swamp. When it came out, the water was fast and muddy.

At good daylight I rowed out with provisions and Sally's clothes in Lou's skiff to get the dinghy. The tide was just turning, and we scrambled aboard. The dinghy was deflated and stowed in the lazaret. The rags went aloft, and I hauled anchor. We had a following breeze and an outgoing current.

# Chapter Thirteen

THE DAY WAS AUGUST 10, 1971. We had been in Gladstone more than a month.

The big ore ships at their mooring slid past the starboard side, but I was giving Sally most of my attention. We had a tape recorder in the cockpit playing new music from the States and were making a party of our sail down the channel and out from behind the island. We passed the sheep island and the old wool pier. Sally thumbed her nose at it. I laughed and looked forward. I saw riffles in the water about two hundred yards ahead. They indicated shoal water, so I jibed her over to take what wind there was on the starboard quarter. By now those riffles had my attention, but it was a little late . . . *Sea Lion* didn't have enough power in her sails to overcome the current. We were being carried right for the shallows!

Suddenly she struck bottom with an awful crunch. What had appeared as riffles were now waves. One lifted her and the current swept her into the thick of it. She struck again and shuddered. Sally freaked out and started breaking out the life jackets. She was trying to get one on Bri. The mate looked at her like she was nuts. I told her to get below and close the portlights. Now *Sea Lion* was lunging up and down as her keel crushed sandstone. Great red billows of mud and sand were all around. Sally wouldn't go below and had frozen in the companionway hatch. I had to jerk her out of the way to get below and secure the portlights. Much water had

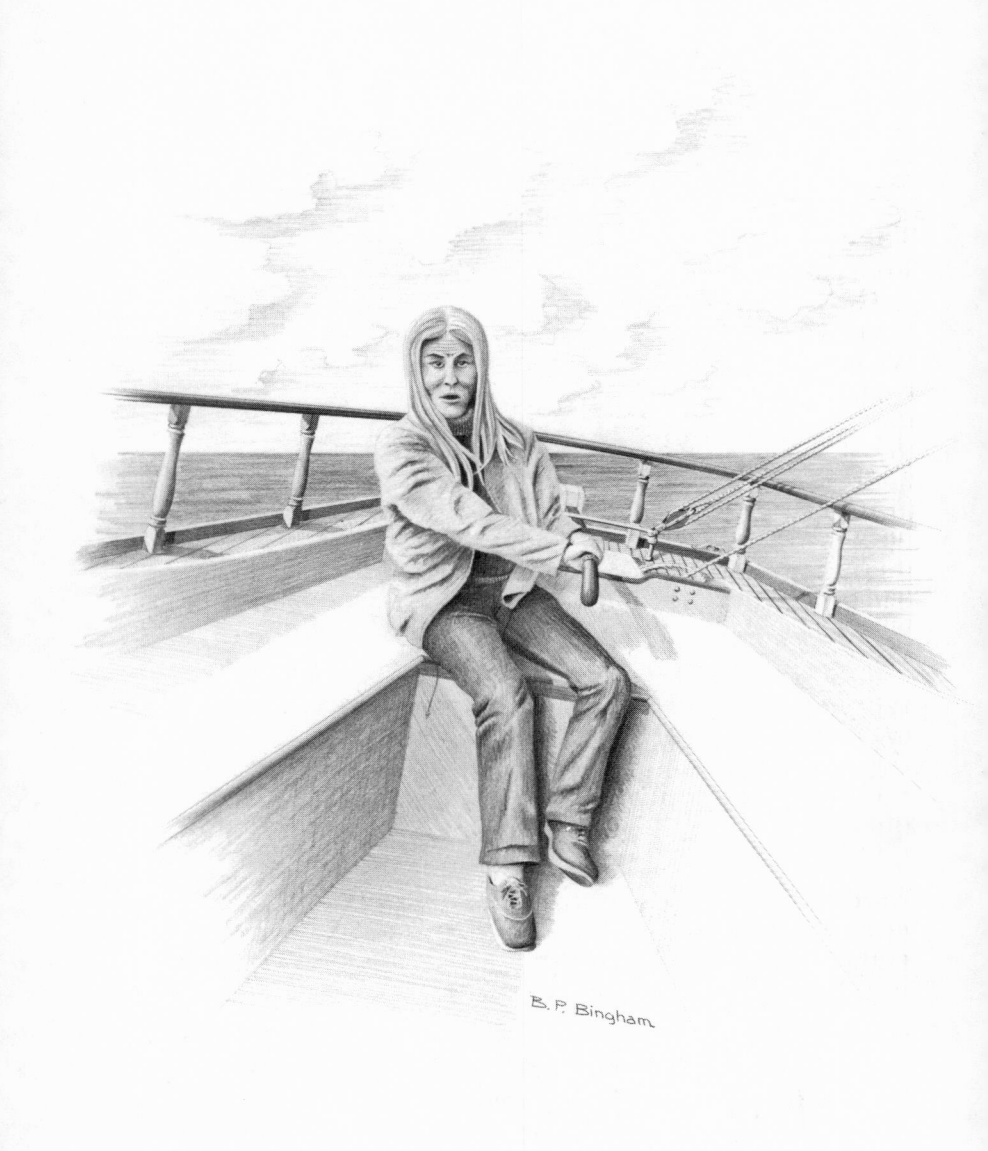

B. P. Bingham

already come in and the bunks were wet. I got back in the cockpit just in time to see Vane Jane tilt crazily off to one side and sink astern! All wind was shaken out of the sails, but I clung to the tiller, trying mostly to keep the rudder from being broken off.

Sally was ashen and clung to the cockpit coaming while Bri tried to comfort her. I could see that the current was carrying us at a fast rate right across the bar. Suddenly the crunching stopped. We bobbed up and down on the current waves, but weren't touching bottom. We had been carried half a mile across the top of that bar. Presently the rags caught a breeze, and she answered the helm. I dashed below and ripped up the cabin sole. There was red muddy water in the bilge. I watched it for breathless moments. No new water was coming in. She wasn't leaking. Sally didn't react to the good news. I had to get her busy at something. With *Sea Lion* on course for Breaksea Spit Lightship, I sat Sally at the tiller. The mate was angry because her pink teddy had got wet! Back below, I sponged the bilge dry. She still wasn't leaking. Sally still wasn't speaking. She sat there woodenly at the tiller.

We had a good northeast breeze and were by now out of the lee of those islands. The Capricorn Group of reefs slipped by in the distance to port. The lightship was in view ahead, and I knew I'd have to cook the meal. Once again, two babies to take care of!

After a batch of spaghetti, Sally felt somewhat better. I kept *Sea Lion* pointed out to deep water. After clearing Breaksea Spit, we turned south down the hundred-fathom line. Sleeping that night was uncomfortable because of the wet bedding. It was just as well for me, since we were still within twenty miles of shore.

The next day Sally was beginning to get some color back in her face, but she was still mighty quiet. She told me she had never been in the open sea before, and said

she thought we'd be in sight of land all the way to Brisbane. I asked her if she didn't think it was nice. She just
stared off out at the sea with her mouth half open. For
hours.

The wind failed that night, but we had a favorable
two-knot current set. I slept some. Sally couldn't sleep
anyway, so I let her stand watch for shipping.

An east wind came with the sun, and we made good
time south. We had seen surprisingly little shipping since
leaving Breaksea Spit, but now we were approaching a
fishing fleet. It was near sundown, and I took the place
to be Barwon Bank. Sally refused to go down into the
cabin at all. Occasionally she fell asleep in the cockpit. I
was worried about her and also a bit angry. She couldn't
even make a pot of coffee. After we'd passed the fishing
boats, the wind hauled around to the north, and I feared
for the poor patched gaff. Sally was to hold the tiller
while I went to get the sail down. She let it jibe and the
bundle of sticks exploded! I got the wreckage down and
the storm trysail back up alone just before the old yankee
jib came apart. It was dark now, and we were moving fast
in the direction we wanted to go, though she rolled badly
with no sail aloft. The fishing vessels quit the bank and
their lights started filing past us. I wondered if they knew
something we didn't. Pieces of conversation were
snatched by the increasing wind from their two-way ra-
dios. As they came up astern, I tried to make out what
was being said, but even when I did hear a word it was
in Aussie. Presently I identified the light from Caloundra
Head. The fishing vessels seemed to be headed in that
direction, so we did too. The wind was starting to howl.
I was very concerned about approaching the entrance to
Moreton Bay in darkness with no local knowledge. I
shouldn't have worried; we weren't going to get there
anyway! At least not this night.

On we flew in the darkness with just the storm jib and
trysail. Those fishing boats seemed to be milling about,

as I would see first the port then the starboard running lights of the same vessel. We were nearing shoal water —the ten-fathom line, by the way the seas were kicking up—when the wind suddenly fell dead. There was not a breath of air! Suddenly great bolts of lightning began zapping into the sea all around! *Blapp! Zorp! Borzzle!* The sound of those mighty arcs of electricity was awesome! I could smell them! That light was so blinding I couldn't see a thing. The image from the previous flash was etched in the brain. It went on for awful moments, sometimes a bolt striking only feet from the gunwale! It sizzled as though a telephone-pole-size hot poker had been thrust in the sea. Just as I was about to leave the tiller to strike sails, we were hit by a blast of wind and knocked down. *Sea Lion* spun around on beam-ends and went screaming away with her bottom for a sail! I clung to the lashed-down boom. I had no idea in what direction we were heading, perhaps the rocks! The rudder was out of the water and Sally was screaming! Frothing seas flew through the taffrail.

Presently the weight of lead in her keel overcame wind, and her sails started to draw. Away she screamed in the night! Lights of fishing boats flew by, scattering in all directions. I just took the wind on the quarter and went where it wanted us to go. Obviously not toward shore, because we would have struck long ago. By daylight there was no sight of land.

Once we were in the open sea, that wind took on a massive quality as the seas grew. The sun was bright, and porpoises surfed all about us. I tried to get Sally to watch them. She kept asking me to tell her we weren't going to die. Bri delighted in the porpoises while I mended the bundle of sticks that was our gaff.

Then it was time to clean the bilge. There were millions of tiny scraps of paper sloshing around in it. They proved to be our passports! All the ship's papers!

Violent motion had caused the big manila envelope to

bounce out of the back of that drawer beneath the starboard bunk. Two more days of it had done the rest.

That night I dropped the flashlight over the side, the one I'd used since Los Angeles. I watched its beam sink in the clear, dark sea.

When the wind did change, it came out of the south. We were two more days clawing west with those rags before we sighted land. At noon that day I took a latitude sight and figured a knob of land to be Noosa Head. None of the Australian "mountains" along the coast are so much as a thousand feet high. Noosa Head showed on the chart to be less than five hundred. We couldn't be far from shore, yet it took most of that day to get in the lee of the headland.

The authorities in Gladstone had told me I was to sail straight to Brisbane, without calling at any other ports. I dropped anchor in thirty feet of clean water about fifty yards off a sandy beach. The south wind was howling high over our heads as *Sea Lion* swung gently to the anchor in an absolute lee. Joy of joys! Even Sally smiled! Bri wanted to go ashore.

The place was some sort of resort. There were a couple of new buildings that looked something like the pub in Gladstone. Sally said she would like to telephone her parents in Brisbane, because we were already overdue. I inflated the dinghy.

There was a good swell running, and I studied the waves before setting out. Timing was nearly right, and the three of us landed on the sand only a little wet. Color came back into Sally's face and she was her old self again. The two of them frolicked down the beach toward the resort.

Re-entering the surf alone was not so smooth. I got soaked. On the second try I made it out, and rowed smartly to *Sea Lion*. There was much patching of sail and cleaning up to be done. It was so great to be alone I

didn't do anything but stretch out in the cockpit and soak up the sunshine, watching the wind fly harmless overhead and strike the water again a hundred yards astern. Lying there, I thought learning to make my own sails out of cotton would be easier than this.

I tuned in the radio to Brisbane. That thing, the storm that had hit us off Caloundra Head, was a tornado! It had killed three people ashore before it pounced on us. There was no mention of any fishing boats being lost. Presently I heard Sally calling from shore. Rowing in to pick them up, I thought that Sally should take a bus on home from here. When I landed, she wouldn't even consider it. Having her feet on land seemed to erase her memory of recent days. We all got a bit wet going back out in that surf, but it was fun.

We lay around patching sails and rigging, and resting, waiting for a favorable wind to enter Moreton Bay. About noon of the third day, it came out of the north. We hauled up anchor and rounded Noosa Head before turning south.

That north wind didn't hold steady. It fanned around out of the west, then pulled southwest. We didn't see any other sailboats. I can understand why. The east coast of Australia is no place to be sailing for fun. At least not in August. It was getting late and I was thinking about going into shoal water to anchor for the night when the wind swung north again and started to blow. We were flying on in toward Moreton Bay, but it was late. I didn't relish the idea of entering that bay in darkness, but there was little choice. The night was coming on fast and would be upon us before we reached the northeast channel.

While studying the chart of Moreton Bay in the fading light, I received a rude shock. I could not focus my eyes to read that small print on the chart identifying the buoy lights. My eyesight had always been excellent and I'd

never worn glasses. It frightened me. The flashlight had gone overboard and the Petromax had a broken glass. I couldn't leave the tiller, and the wind was increasing. Darkness came on. I sent Sally below to read the chart by the dim cabin lamps. That's when I discovered she could not read a chart! I had just assumed that she could because she was working crew on the ferryboat. Well, we were in it by now and fast approaching an array of blinking red and green lights. I'd pick out one and scream out the sequence of light and dark while Sally tried to find it on the chart.

Moreton Bay is very large, especially at the entrance. Although wide, the entire entrance is covered with shoals, banks, and drifting channels. No large vessel would dare enter without a pilot who was aware of yesterday's change in the bottom. The chart showed the positions of several hulks that hadn't made it, even with pilots.

*Sea Lion* drew only four feet, and I wasn't too worried till I saw white water breaking in the darkness to port. I had no idea what state the tide was in, and there were places on the chart that showed only one fathom (six feet) at low tide. The wind began to howl and navigation lights scudded past, blinking a message that told me nothing. We had missed the evening meal because Sally couldn't prime and light the stove. I was tired, angry, and very disturbed by not being able to see the chart. Then more white water breaking to starboard! Finally I abandoned any effort to steer by the navigation aids and just helped *Sea Lion* avoid the breaking areas. We were really flying into I knew not what! Cold came with the darkness, and I began to lose circulation in my hands and feet. If only. If only I had a cup of hot coffee and honey.

I pleaded with Sally to make coffee as she stood in the companionway begging me to tell her we were not going to die. Bri was asleep on the lee bunk. I made out the

lights of a large ship crossing our course. That must be the dredged channel. Not bothering to come about, I ran forward on numb feet and fumbled to release the anchor. The anchor line spewed out and I let it run, knowing the bitter end was secured below. She hit the end of three hundred feet of nylon while I was in midair jumping back down into the cockpit. I landed on the cockpit seat and the taffrail gave me a hell of a blow to the ribs right under my right arm. She swung up into the wind to answer the anchor warp. I threw off all halyards and let the rags fall where they damn well pleased. That big ship's lights passed at about fifty yards, now off our stern.

I went below, shoved Sally aside, and fired up the stove. Soon the cabin was warm. Sally calmed down, and the circulation came tingling back to my hands and feet. We had a bowl of hot soup each while Bri slept on. Another ship's lights passed our stern at fifty yards, and I knew the anchor was holding. I slept in fits sitting on the companionway ladder. Sometime before daylight fatigue played one of its tricks. I went out in the cockpit to the tiller. It was dead amidships. My leg touched it and *Sea Lion* instantly answered! I grabbed hold and swung it the other way; she romped off on that course. I screamed in the darkness, "By God, we're sailing!" I looked up and there were no sails. So what? We were flying through the water! I put the helm hard over to come about and she did! Away we flew on the other tack! I went below to tell Sally the great news. We had discovered unlimited power, perpetual motion, without sails! She stared at me in her catatonic state and said, "Just tell me we're not going to die." That sobered me some, and when I went back out in the cockpit, it was cracking daylight. Alas, we had not found perpetual motion. We were hung on three hundred feet of nylon warp in shoal water in a tremendous current flowing in the same direction as a strong wind.

Bri woke up hungry, and I cooked porridge. With the warm food in my belly, I began to realize that all this power of wind and current was flowing in our favor toward Brisbane. And there we were, tied to the bottom! The chart showed—now that I had light—that we were anchored on the edge of Spitfire Banks.

I went forward and took the anchor line in hand. It wouldn't budge. It was as stiff as a steel rod running out into the sea! There was no winch on *Sea Lion.* I went back below and broke out a quart jar of pure honey. I told Sally to take the tiller. With the jar of honey in hand, I went forward. After several large gulps of thick honey, I closed the lid, laid the jar in a pile of ragged sails on the cabin top, and motioned for Sally to put the helm hard over. *Sea Lion* roared away on a "cabin reach," and I grabbed the slack in the anchor line and took a turn on the samson post. Sally put it hard over the other way, and I got a bit more. As the line shortened, little or nothing could be gained by the tiller. After three more large gulps of honey, I started taking in the line a foot at a time. I'd pull a bight of line straight up and snatch the slack on the samson post. By the time I had gulped over a pint of honey, the anchor line was standing nearly up and down. I was on my knees panting. I couldn't pull another time. I just stared at the stiff vertical line. Suddenly it broke free!

Now it was a scramble to get sail up. With the muddy anchor aboard, *Sea Lion* sizzled away toward the entrance to Brisbane River. It was happy time again. Unfortunately, the wind fell off about halfway there and that inflowing current went slack. With light airs, it was sundown before we reached the quarantine anchorage at the entrance of the Brisbane River. Making sure we were within the dotted lines on the chart, I dropped the anchor in six fathoms of muddy water. I was exhausted. I told them both to feed themselves, and went to sleep

with instructions not to be wakened under any circumstances.

I heard them puttering about the galley and soon went into a deep sleep. Suddenly I was being shaken and screamed at! Sally was in a panic! I dashed out in the cockpit to see a gigantic tanker bearing down on us! The tanker was empty and rose several stories out of the water. I pointed out to Sally the lights of Pile Lighthouse just off the quarantine anchorage, and explained that the ship was on the proper course and only appeared to be bearing down on us. She threw a fit and insisted we take up anchor and move! I threw a fit, threatening to do her bodily harm if she woke me again, and went below to sleep.

When I woke the next morning, the two were asleep on the other bunk. I made coffee and studied what charts we had with eyes that could see a bit better after sleep. We had no chart for the river itself. I didn't want to take a shaky lady up a river I knew nothing about. There was a jetty on the chart we did have, with a town called Redcliffe behind it. Before she woke I had decided to put Sally ashore there. I pulled anchor and raised sails, which woke them. I asked Sally if she knew of a town called Redcliffe. She said she did. I told her to pack her things, that I was putting her ashore there. It was a silent and lonesome sail over to that jetty. With *Sea Lion* tied up, we went ashore. Sally went to a phone to call her parents. She came back to us and said it was a long way for them to come by car; she pleaded to continue on up the river on *Sea Lion*. Of course, she was ashore now and very confident. I felt like some kind of jerk, so we went back aboard *Sea Lion* and cast off for Brisbane. We were now twelve days out of Gladstone on a trip that should have taken four.

By taking a short cut, we intersected the channel well upstream from Pile Lighthouse and the quarantine an-

chorage. By now the tide was flowing back in and we fairly scooted up the river in darkness. The channel was well marked with lights but dogleg crooked.

In the wee hours tide was at flood and slack. The wind died. A tanker bore down on us. Its whistle hooted. While Sally held the lantern to light the sails, I rowed with the dinghy paddle. That giant ship never changed course or speed and *Sea Lion* rose on the swell of displaced water. It actually pushed us safely clear. The pulsating monster hooted and slid on down the dark river.

The tide turned before daylight, and there was no wind. *Sea Lion* found some good mud for her anchor over to the side of the marked channel. With sunrise we could see that there was a lot of heavy industry on both sides of the river. The water was filthy. An ore ship was unloading just ahead, and two more waited. There was quite a current flowing and not enough wind to overcome it. I went to sleep while Bri and Sally watched the parade of heavy shipping pass. Early in the afternoon the current was flowing in with a beam wind that lasted till dark. We made good time but had difficulty staying clear of shipping. As the current reversed, we anchored right next to Brisbane's electric generating plant. The deep, throbbing sound of gigantic generators was awesome. I could feel the flux, or magnetic field.

About halfway through tide change, a patrol boat came alongside. It had twin outboards and I'd seen it in the river before but had no idea it was official. There were two young officers, and they asked if we were in distress. Well, no. No, thank you, we don't need a tow. I asked them how far it was up the river to Norm Wright's boatyard. We were only slightly over halfway there and had already been in the river two days! They showed me how to find it on their chart and shoved off with best wishes.

That soft, silty mud in the riverbed was not good holding ground. *Sea Lion*'s foredeck was stained a charcoal

color, and washing down with the filthy river water made it worse.

⁂ On the fifteenth day out of Gladstone we came to a ninety-degree turn in the river with inflowing current and a good following breeze. In spite of her rags, *Sea Lion* was stepping out smartly. I spotted Norm Wright's yard on the left bank. There was a small anchorage off the ways. Three or four small craft were hanging on moorings streamed out in the incoming current. *Sea Lion* flew amongst them. I spotted a small camera crew on one of the neighboring piers. They were operating a 16-mm. motion-picture camera. It appeared to be a news crew. We were moving fast with all rags flying. I picked a spot, ran forward, and dumped the anchor. Line ran out. I snubbed it off and dashed to the halyards. When *Sea Lion* hit the end of anchor warp, she swapped ends and the rags came down. As I watched the anchor line to be sure we were holding, a skiff came rowing out. The passenger was a reporter for the local TV station. After a short interview, he informed us the footage would be on the news that night. It was now about three-thirty in the afternoon on August 25, 1971. After the reporter had gone, I tried to tell Sally to calm down, I didn't see how they could have that film ready for the evening newscast. Sally and Bri scrambled to get their clothes packed to take a cab and not miss the broadcast. After I rowed them ashore and returned in the dinghy, fatigue overcame me.

Norm Wright's was truly an old-time "timber" boatyard. There were two large marine railways, and one small one. At the time I was there, they were laying the keel for a ninety-foot vessel. There was a high false front on the building bearing faded letters of the firm's name. It reminded me of a "Western" storefront. Norm himself was deceased, and a son was the architect in residence. In the days that followed I had access to a hallowed museum. Those steep steps up to the drafting loft were

nearly three-inch timber worn to a quarter inch at the front edge. Photographs and half models of a century's production of wooden vessels covered the office walls.

Those half models of Norm Wright's successful eighteen-foot racers reminded me of *Libra*'s lines. I studied them for hours. The atmosphere in that yard was a place to dream. I roamed the yard and rested for days while Bri enjoyed home life with Sally's parents.

Brisbane itself gave me the feeling that I had sailed into Oklahoma City of about 1930. Generally the people were gruff and unfriendly.

I found a sailmaker and ordered a new suit of sails. Only Dacron was available. They called it Terylene. The price was reasonable but production not rapid. Because I had no gaff spar, we laid out the ragged pieces of the old mainsail on the ground and took measurements. Not an accurate method. I decided not to haul out. *Sea Lion* wasn't leaking after what I felt had been a thorough test. It was a tough decision, because I couldn't replace Vane Jane otherwise. Actually I was just too tired.

Each district had its pub. They were always in a hotel. The pub on Norm Wright's side of the river was a new building. Most of its customers were workers in meat-packing plants along the river. The main pump room in that pub was as large as—and had the acoustics of—a gymnasium. It was tile-floored, with drains, and the walls were tile to shoulder height. A six-inch shelf, chest high, ran around the entire arena. One day I happened to be walking past at noon. I heard an ominous sound three blocks away. By the time I passed across the street, it was a snarling roar. This was lunch hour and there were thousands of bicycles parked outside. More thousands of men were inside drinking their lunch. I had never heard anything like it. I've been to big zoos. I've heard river rapids and mud slides. Even bawling herds of thirsty cattle wouldn't compare.

I crossed the street and went in. The sound was mind-boggling. Four bars stuck out into the crowd like piers. Shouting men stood six deep at all the bars and passed sloshing glasses of brew back to their "mates," who waded in beer the drains couldn't handle. At least twenty barpeople poured and collected. Suddenly a loud buzzer went off, there was a stampede, and the place emptied! I asked for a beer and my voice echoed in the empty gym.

Some days I took a cab to Sally's parents' home. Bri had moved in. Mama was a lovely lady. Dad had lost interest. I dug them a garden plot in the back yard. Down on my hands and knees digging out grass roots made me landsick. How to make a living? Sally wouldn't go to sea, but told me she'd like to try it on some dirt. We looked at a few places, but I didn't see anything that would make me stay in Australia.

Finally the four-by-four of Oregon pine arrived at the yard. I began to shape a new gaff. My methods for fashioning the spar were far from orthodox. The yard workmen watched me and grinned. After cutting tapering excess off the four-by-four with a radial saw, I used a hand plane to shape the timber down to tapers from the center, leaving the bottom edge straight. In three days it made a very respectable spar. In the meantime I was daily pestering the sailmaker to finish. It was time to leave Australia. Low on funds, I remembered the money owed me for work on that powerboat back in Gladstone. I located the real-estate developer and presented a list of tackle needed to make us seaworthy. There was no argument; he said I should simply go to a certain marine supply store and pick out what I needed.

With the stack of goodies on the counter, that store informed me the tycoon hadn't paid his bill. I flipped. I was still flipping when I got his man on the phone. I did manage to get me a new mainsheet, a spare anchor, and a good waterproof flashlight.

Sally was a different person ashore. One night she took me out to see the night life of Brisbane. It reminded me of a 1940s movie. The gangsters all wore pin-stripe suits with knit ties and snap-brim hats. They drove big black cars and swaggered.

I knew I didn't want to stay in Australia, but I didn't know where to go. Perhaps New Zealand. I still had their twenty-dollar bill. The Tasman Sea had always fascinated me in old salts' stories. Along with Cape Hatteras, it had a reputation for natural fierceness. Natural fierceness seemed much more attractive than what I was likely to encounter to the north.

Australia had sponsored an immigration program for years. Thank God they got some Italians. I found their ghetto in Brisbane and replenished our stores with fine paṣta and sauce. They also had the only coffee beans worth taking aboard.

The sails were delivered and fitted poorly. They were cut flat, as though we wanted to race *Sea Lion* to windward. I wasn't about to hang around for another set, even if I'd had the money.

On a Friday we'd been in Brisbane a month. One shouldn't sail on a Friday. I requested clearance of the harbor on Monday. On that day a proper authority came out to *Sea Lion* in a skiff very early in the morning. He cleared us for sailing.

With Briewfn as sole crew, we hauled anchor at sunrise and caught the ebb tide at 2100 GMT on September 27, 1971. With favorable winds, *Sea Lion* flew down that river as though flushed by the toilets of Brisbane. By nightfall we were approaching North Point on Moreton Island, having covered a distance that had taken us four days on entering!

# Chapter Fourteen

WE WERE BOUND for New Zealand. It was a nine-day run, but *Sea Lion* was provisioned for at least thirty. With Cape Moreton Light still on the starboard quarter, the waves became those of deepwater seas. With Brennan and Roberts shoals still ahead, there'd be no sleep. I tucked a reef in the main and struck the staysail. There wasn't much wind, but I was determined not to have the new sails blown off. It was a lonely watch. I missed Vane Jane, and was to miss her more. I wasn't too worried, because my good-luck charm slept soundly on the lee bunk. She hadn't thrown her usual fit on this departure. She was growing up. Too fast. I knew that in less than a year it would require a full-time hand to prevent her from taking unnecessary chances, just for the thrill of it. Sally and her mother had not stuffed the child with candy as had other "mamas." My first mate was strong and healthy at the beginning of this departure.

Sunrise brought a fresh southwest breeze, and *Sea Lion* romped away to the east. With the staysail back up and full main, I eased the sheets and just let her find her course. From the start there was something ominous about this sea. Perhaps it was my state of mind. By sundown I was nauseated. I'd never been seasick in my life, so couldn't be sure I was now. If so, it tended to confirm a notion I had that seasickness is the expression of fear . . . sometimes very deeply buried. I shortened sail at sunset and went to bed early. The wind had shifted from

PROTRON

PROTRON

B.P. Bingham

southeast, so I let her make east while we both got a good sleep.

Sunrise came with a light east-southeast breeze. We made south under an overcast sky. With the portable radio's RDF help, I guesstimated our position to be 170 miles east-southeast of Brisbane.

It was our third day out. We baked bread and read *Scuppers, the Sailor Dog*. My uneasy stomach of the day before was gone. Even though the wind remained light out of the east-southeast, those seas did not settle down. They seemed to have massive life independent of the wind. I shortened sail again at dark to get another lovely rest.

Morning broke clear, though we were almost becalmed. I got sun fixes for our position as three black birds paddled along in *Sea Lion*'s slight wake. We continued to make south through the night.

On the morning of October 1 the wind pulled around to come out of the north at about Force 3. Sun was bright and warm. An almost perfect day. By nightfall the wind was increasing and beginning to swing to northwest. I tucked three reefs in the main and struck the yankee jib. By daylight that was all the sail she could carry! Seas were getting high and cross as that wind cranked up out of the northwest. *Sea Lion* was flying southeast with the tiller lashed. Those three black seabirds swam in our wake, flying low occasionally to catch up, then swimming hard and fast to hold their gain. Soon I had to take the tiller in hand. We were taking wind and seas dead astern. Gradually the wind increased to gale! In order to make supper we hove to. She would not do so with reefed sails, and I had to shake two of them out and raise the jib. The seas were becoming monstrous. *Sea Lion* bobbed over most of them ducklike, only occasionally taking a solid one against the cabin. Bri was clowning as we ate supper squatting on the cabin sole. She was pitched forward into

the mast and busted her nose. It bled a little, and she cried herself to sleep, clutching the pink teddy.

I slept fitfully on the weather bunk through the night as the gale seemed to increase. By daylight those three black birds were still paddling about in our lee. Bri's nose was only slightly puffed while we ate pancakes.

As the gray light increased, so did the wind. It was at least Force 8 by now, and the leech was being popped off that new main! I decided to try and sail in it. After an hour's struggle to get three reefs back in the main and the staysail struck, I took the tiller in hand and ran off before it. The seas were big. *Sea Lion* was carrying too much sail, too low. It took all my strength to keep her nose downwind. We fought it for about three hours before I gave up. The main went back up with the jib and we hove to again. At least our leeway was on course. Suddenly the peak halyard parted! Worst of all, the block aloft had been carried away! Instead of heaving to properly, she now wallowed off on a kind of reach, shipping large seas into the cockpit.

Gradually the wind abated with fading light. I struck the main and let her wallow off downwind under headsails. After supper I hunted around on the shortwave band for some music. I got a report from Sydney that a sixty-foot sailing vessel had sunk in the Tasman. As the report unfolded to give its position relative to Lord Howe Island, I knew that we were not more than ten miles from it. There were five people in a raft somewhere out in this! A massive search was being organized. I felt a surge of pride in *Sea Lion*'s hull. The larger vessel had opened seams in this same blow and gone to the bottom in fifteen minutes!

The following morning we were becalmed. Seas remained high. I contented myself with sewing a new leech on the main, waiting for the seas to calm to go aloft to replace the block.

Briewfn was tickled to have a chance to be all over me.

We listened to the radio reports of the search for those
five souls on a raft. Vessels of three navies were par-
ticipating. I worried about being run down by one of
them, since we were so close to the scene. With the main
patched, I had to go aloft even if the seas were still high.
*Sea Lion* was thrashing from side to side and the mast
whipped back and forth. I watched it till afternoon, and
then went up the ratlines with block and shackle in hand.
I knew there would be no second chance if I slipped and
fell. It was a difficult job because the block was to be
secured above the point where the shrouds intersected
the mast. I had to climb the whipping pole! Then work!
Deck was only thirty feet below but *Sea Lion* looked tiny.
Suddenly I heard a roaring sound! I looked about frantically and saw a giant flying boat approaching just off the
water! It was a big four-engine seaplane roaring past at
eye level not fifty yards off the starboard! It circled. I was
afraid the monster might think we needed assistance and
sink us when it landed! I scrambled back on deck and
struck a carefree lounging attitude in the cockpit as it
continued to circle. We could plainly see the pilot. I
tossed him a careless wave and told Bri to throw him a
kiss. It worked. Soon he took a westerly course and disappeared over the horizon.

In no hurry to go aloft again, I aired bedding. I tuned
in to get news of the search. The five were still missing.
U.S. Navy submarines had joined in the search. I put a
pot of beans on for supper and went back aloft to thread
halyard through blocks, all the while looking about for
the raft or for a rescue vessel to run us down. I looked
aft and saw my mattress sitting on the waves. It was
always damp anyway, and we'd already lost a third of
Bri's. I slept in the sleeping bag on wood, always tired
enough to be comfortable.

It was just as well that I hadn't waited for the seas to
calm; they never did.

By night the rigging and main were ready, but caught

only a slight easterly breeze at sunup. Before I finished coffee, there were mackerel clouds in the eastern sky. A fresh breeze came out of the north-northwest and increased. Three reefs were tucked in the main and the jib struck.

By sunup it was blowing a good Force 5. Those three black birds had increased to about fifty. They must have been natives of Lord Howe Island. I shook the reef out and raised the jib. *Sea Lion* was doing hull speed, and the flock stayed about twenty yards astern all that day. They leapfrogged over each other in groups of flight. We continued to make south, the plan being to get down to New Zealand's latitude, then head east till we came upon it. I would hate to miss it. There was nothing else this side of Chile and no turning back against the "roaring forties." The radio said they still hadn't found those five in the raft. There was little hope, but the search was continuing.

Wind stayed favorable all the next day until late afternoon. It switched rather suddenly to come out of the southwest. The birds took flight. They flew back to the west low over the water and out of sight.

The next day was October 6. We were ten days out of Brisbane and had been on the voyage exactly one year this morning. It was also the captain's birthday, and I couldn't focus to read anything small within arm's reach. I cursed it!

The chart used was still that one covering the South Pacific from the Marquesas to Australia, including the Tasman Sea and New Zealand. Only in bright sunlight could I make out the smaller print on the Pilot chart. I could see the red lines quite clearly. Storms born in the Coral Sea head off southeast for Cape Horn. The Tasman Sea catches the outside edge of those counterclockwise rotations. Winds of eighty knots are common, generally out of the northwest.

The wind remained out of the southwest and we held to an easterly course. About this time I noticed two very large birds soaring over our wake some distance astern. At first they appeared as airplanes in the distance . . . but that was probably because I'd watched so intently for search craft. The five people were still not found, and there was talk on the radio of calling it off. Those two birds remained astern and out of scale until darkness hid them. The wind failed in the night. Stars were hidden in overcast. I lit the lantern for a stern light. *Sea Lion* was barely ghosting come daylight.

As I went on deck with the first cup of coffee, there was one flying fish and a squid lying in the cockpit. They must have flown at the lantern. I was too tired to cook them. I took it as a good omen and offered them to the two giant birds. First I tossed the flying fish into the wake. It was amazing how these birds could remain flying in such light airs. As *Sea Lion* crept away from the floating fish, one of those giants spotted it from afar and came in for a landing. It was an albatross. The first I'd ever seen. A giant albatross. Its landing was downright comical. Suddenly giant webbed feet stuck out, and those graceful wings broke in the middle and thrashed backwards. It hit the water with a great splash. With wings held aloft, it swam toward the dead fish. By now the second one was circling close. From book learning I could tell it was a mallemuck—somewhat smaller than the giant albatross and perfectly marked with black and white. The giant was tricolored over white. It had a buff underbelly, black on its wings, and two distinct reddish-brown eyebrows. As I tossed the squid in the wake, Bri came out of the cabin. The mallemuck landed right in front of that swimming giant to scoop up the morsel. It was the first time Bri had taken an interest in anything over the gunwale without my saying "Look yonder." She was delighted and wanted to name them. She asked what they were. "I want the

black-and-white one. His name is Albert. Albert Tross."

"Okay, kid. I'll take the big one. He's Brownie
McGee."

Later she added the initial "J" to her bird's name.
Brownie McGee and Albert J. Tross finally gave up on
any more morsels being tossed in the wake and decided
to get airborne. With their wings held aloft and folded
at the "elbow," they waited for the next large swell.
Albert J. Tross thought it would do and began flapping
those long wings and running across the water's surface
to meet it. Brownie McGee wanted a bigger one. There
was practically no wind. Those birds weighed between
twenty and thirty pounds. Albert ran up the face of that
swell flapping mightily. Suddenly he was airborne and
continued to beat his mighty wings low over the water.
Another swell came, and he seemed to have intentions
of flying right into it. Suddenly he shot straight up with
outstretched wings! He had caromed off the air cushion
being forced in front of the wave.

There is a saying that every seventh wave is larger.
Well, that's not always true, but it's close. Brownie
picked a big one and started running across the water.
His big feet sent up great splashes. Those wings of his
must have been sixteen feet, tip to tip. He too caromed
off the air cushion and went aloft. After they were in the
air, they seldom flapped their wings.

Tuning in Sydney to get news of the search was a main
event. About noon we heard that the search had been
abandoned. Visibility had been bad for days, with very
high seas. The Tasman just doesn't settle down after a
blow, and mostly it's blowing. Great conditions for albatross. Bri watched the two soaring about us till dark.

We saw the sun at noon the next day. Latitude 33°
44'. We were nearing the New Zealand parallel, which is
34° S.

That afternoon we heard a report that the raft with five

people had been found by a submarine. Five days in a
raft. In the Tasman. The rescued people said they had
seen search vessels several times for days. They had even
fired flares and put dye in the water. There was much talk
on the radio about making the rescued pay for the
search!

Being October, it was early spring "down under." I
shortened sail at dark and, sure enough, the wind pulled
around out of the northwest and started to blow. I remained at the tiller all night to try and take advantage of
the force. We held an easterly course, allowing nothing
to north. By daylight it was blowing a full gale. There
were two reefs in the main and the staysail was struck, but
it was all I could do to keep her nose downwind. Those
seas had built during the night, and were truly monstrous by midmorning. *Sea Lion* had shipped considerable water. I was tired. We hove to for a rest and bilge
pumping. It was hard to keep Bri below. She wanted to
watch Albert J. Tross and Brownie McGee. They were in
their element with this weather. As the vessel bobbed
over those gigantic seas, hove to with the wind on her
port bow, the two birds circled in escort. Bri watched
them from the ladder. We were making good time to
leeward. After a couple of hours' rest, I decided to try
sailing. With three reefs in the main and the storm jib
alone, she was all I could handle! I surely missed Vane
Jane and wondered how I could have been so lazy and
cheap as not to replace her in Brisbane. It was necessary
to heave to for supper. I was exhausted and left her hove
to for sleep that night. Occasionally the vessel would get
herself crossways and catch a "green one" smack against
the cabin. It didn't happen often, but always woke me.
Nothing woke Bri.

By daylight the sky was clear, though the wind howled
on. I was getting desperate to know our longitude. It's
possible to observe sunrise and interpolate longitude,

though I had been warned by Bernard that it was inaccurate, especially in high seas, but it was all I had. When the sun peeked up, I noted the exact time and worked it out. I got 171°E. Hell, New Zealand was at 172! We were thirteen days out of Brisbane—plenty of time to cover the distance—yet I knew we'd had to "park" for each meal and several whole nights. In any event, I was struck with the possibility of having the west coast of New Zealand for a lee shore tomorrow! That sun was only visible on rising. There was no morning sight, but I did manage to get a doubtful noon latitude. 34°17'S. The wind died and there were signs of a change. I dreaded that, because the seas were high from two days of gale out of the northwest. There were great mare's tails fanning up out of the south and west. In an hour the wind came. Out of the west-southwest at gale force! The seas went wild! At times like this I'd just put out cheese, crackers, and dried fruit where the mate could get at it, slide the companionway hatch closed, leaving one door open to see each other, and go to the tiller.

The wind was a bit colder coming from the south. To go below for extra clothing, I just slacked the sheets, lashed the tiller slightly to weather, and let her romp along on a loose reach. Knowing I would have to be at the tiller through the night, I remained below and visited with the mate. The compass was visible low under the tiller, but I had to read the reverse of our course. All hell was breaking loose out there while we chatted and munched cheese and crackers. The ride got rough in an hour or two as the seas built out of the southwest to cross the ones left from northwest. We were making more south than I wanted to, so I went to take the tiller in hand. *Sea Lion* was full reefed and thrashing through the seas. All through the night I strained to see into the darkness ahead. Finally daylight came and we had not struck a lee shore. The wind pulled around west and

increased. I held it dead astern for a couple of hours, but it got too hairy. We hove to, and I went below for coffee and fixed the mate porridge. It started to rain hard. The cabin leaked under strain. What bedding remained was already damp; now it got soggy. I knew we must have made fifty or sixty miles during the night. My only information indicated that we would soon run aground on the west coast of New Zealand. It was blowing a gale and visibility was zero. Bri, ignorant of the situation, demanded that I read *Scuppers, the Sailor Dog.* I did.

After a while the seas began to smooth, although the wind still raged. About noon the rain stopped and the wind pulled back to southwest and abated. I shook a reef out and raised the yankee. We were flying again. The wind held at a good Force 5. Visibility was good; still no New Zealand. There was no sun. Suddenly Brownie McGee swooped low over the mast. Albert J. Tross followed. They had stayed with us through the blow. My spirits lifted with their soaring! God, they were magnificent! Once Brownie flew into the lee of the mainsail. There was no wind there, and he had to flap his giant wings. His feet came down as if to land. He was suddenly very ungraceful. Bri hollered with laughter. Just as he was about to hit the water, he caught the wind and returned to grace.

We had beans and corn bread for supper. There was corn bread left over, and I pitched a chunk into the wake. The two albatrosses immediately splashed down and had a foot race for it! They followed swimming in the wake as Bri doled out the remaining corn bread. Surely we would raise the sight of land before dark. We didn't.

I spent the night at the tiller. The log entry for the next day, October 11, 1971, was, "Where the hell is New Zealand?" The plastic sextant had a fair assortment of filters, and I managed to get a noon latitude sight of 34°32'S. Well below the north tip of North Island of New

Zealand. Had we passed it? Could we somehow have
sailed right past the Three Kings, those islands off the
north tip? By this time fatigue had me on the ropes. Only
the thought of plank splintering on rocks kept me conscious the rest of that day. The mate had learned to give
me a wide berth when I was in such a state, and played
contentedly with her pink teddy on the cabin sole. We
had long since covered the distance to New Zealand from
my last estimation of longitude. The wind continued at
Force 5 out of the southwest. I hove to for supper, and
we had spaghetti, but I baked a batch of corn bread for
Albert and Brownie at the mate's insistence. It was some
sixty hours since I'd slept. With *Sea Lion* hove to, I
crashed on the lee bunk while the mate tossed corn
bread to her birds.

Ten hours later we were flying again, still riding the
southwest wind. By now I was almost certain we had
somehow missed New Zealand and were on our way
across the roaring forties to Santiago, Chile. At least I
was rested. At noon I managed to "squeeze" a noon
latitude sight out of the haze. 34°59'S. By interpolation
the longitude came out 169°E! I knew we couldn't be
going backward, but that's all I knew. I spent the rest of
that day at the tiller heading east at hull speed, between
five and six knots. As suppertime approached, the wind
pulled south and fell off some. It was now possible to lash
the tiller with the staysail sheeted flat and three reefs in
the main and hold an easterly course. I don't recall what
we ate that evening, but I'm sure Brownie and Albert had
corn bread.

About half convinced we were on our way across the
vast South Pacific toward Chile, I slept through the night
in reasonable comfort.

At sunup we were becalmed. The sky was still overcast
and seas high. Albert and Brownie were caroming off the
waves and cavorting about at leisure. Those two were

something to behold! Without a breath of wind they soared! Brownie, the giant albatross, differed from Albert, the mallemuck, in many ways. Whereas Albert's tail feathers were used as a rudder, Brownie used his toes. They stuck aft beyond his feathers and had the appearance of human feet. Ten toes with nails, pink and extremely dexterous. Albert had the face of a bird. Brownie was almost human in his expressions and markings. A chocolate-brown grin enhanced his reddish eyebrows. The two would soar in the dead air, losing altitude until the last moment, then pick a breaking wave and carom off its face to shoot straight up a hundred feet! Then the soaring would begin, utilizing the very nth-degree glide angle till the next big wave, never once flapping their wings.

A breeze came up out of the south, about Force 2. I shook two reefs out of the main and hoisted the yankee jib. She ran east with a free helm. With this breeze the two winged creatures put on an aerial show that held the mate and me speechless. Brownie McGee seemed to love the thrill of swooping into the vacuum behind the mainsail. Perhaps it was his audience's response that made him do it again, and again, until our sides ached with laughter.

Presently other albatrosses joined the two. There were giants and mallemucks. At first just a few, then many. Each of the giant albatrosses had distinct and individual markings, while the mallemucks were all exactly alike in their formal black and white. We could pick out Albert only because he stayed near Brownie. Those expressions on the giants' faces were limitless! Leering, laughing, sad, and hateful. Soon the air was filled with seabirds of every description!

Had Brownie not swooped low to port I would not have seen the first ship since Brisbane. It was a freighter, hull down on an easterly course. I wondered if she was

bound for Auckland or Santiago. We had not seen the
sun clearly for six days. I kept the sextant and stopwatch
handy in the cockpit, just in case.

At noon I managed to get a hazy sun on the horizon
for a latitude fix. 34°24′S. The estimated longitude came
out 171°30′E, but I had no confidence in it. The wind fell
to less than one from the south and the sky cleared after
nightfall. The full moon rose to give high seas a ghostly
quality. There was barely enough wind to hold steerage.
I was wondering if it would be possible to shoot the
moon for a fix with that ghostly horizon when there came
an awesome sound.

It came from afar. From aft. Out of the Tasman. Bri
was below, and I assumed asleep. At first I dismissed it
as imagination. The sound grew. A deep roar! As the
ominous roar increased in volume, I strained to see out
into the ghostly moonlight. I saw a white line from horizon to horizon coming fast toward us. By now the roar
was joined by a hissing. An enormous wave, breaking all
along its crest! We were dead in the water and the thing
was coming fast. I could do nothing but hold the lifeless
tiller and watch it come. *Sea Lion* was broadside to it, and
we would surely broach! It all happened very fast, because the thing was moving about sixty knots. Suddenly
the sails filled. That monstrous wave was less than a
hundred yards off and closing. We were being sucked
back into it, but the effect was of sailing. The tiller came
to life, and *Sea Lion* swung her stern toward it just as Bri
came scrambling out of the cabin. She said, "God al-
mighty, Papa, look at that son of a bitch!" and up the face
we went! I recall the feeling of an elevator ride, holding
the tiller with both hands, its after end pointing straight
up to the moon! Bri let out a "Wheeee!" as *Sea Lion*
popped over the frothing crest. She stood watching forward over the cabin. *Sea Lion* slid down the back of that
monster wave, leaving a fizzling line of bubbles in the

moonlight. Not a drop of water came aboard. I watched aft for the next one. There was no next one. I've never seen anything like it before or since.

The rest of that night we just ghosted north and south across a light easterly breeze. The next day it was much the same in the company of many birds. There were seabirds I'd never seen before cavorting with the albatrosses. We imagined a couple of times that we saw Brownie, but there were so many! It was October 16. We got a morning and noon fix! The first in ten days! 35° 04'S by 171°10'E. We hadn't passed New Zealand after all! It must be just over the horizon, but there was little wind. We were a bit south of the tip of North Island, so I tried to make as much north as possible the rest of that day. Bri fed a flock of birds cheese as they swam in the slight wake. They acted just like a flock of chickens. Knowing land was close, I slept in short naps, sometimes sitting up. The wind pulled around from the northeast with nightfall. It remained light, and an overcast blocked out the moon and stars. Well into the night I saw a light. It was off the port bow. I watched its pattern. Reinga Point Light. Range, thirty miles! Nineteen days out of Brisbane! I almost woke Bri to celebrate, but it started to rain lightly and visibility fell.

All the next day it drizzled rain and visibility remained low, but I didn't mind. I knew where we were! The west coast of New Zealand was inching by some twenty miles to starboard as we worked our way back and forth across light northeast breezes.

The mate wanted to know where the birds went when it rained. What did they eat if we didn't feed them? Did they sleep in the air on their wings? Or just on the water? Huh? I was exhausted by nightfall. That night the "old lady" came out of her case. It was the first time I'd taken the instrument in hand for many months. I didn't really know how to play it, but had put the thing aboard along

with Pete Seeger's *How to Play the Five-String Banjo* just in
case I ran out of anything to do on the voyage. This night
it was a great aid in keeping me awake between tacks in
those light airs. By daylight I had learned to play "Crip-
ple Creek," very slowly.

The wind, what little there was, had swung around out
of the north. I assumed we were by now at least on the
latitude of Reinga Light, if not a bit farther north and
toward the Three Kings Islands. *Sea Lion* took an easterly
heading and ghosted along with a free helm while we had
pancakes. Before the breakfast dishes were finished, that
wind had fallen off till we barely had steerage. A dense
fog set in. We were sitting in the shipping lane between
Australia and New Zealand. Here it is a narrow lane
because ships pass between the Three Kings and Cape
Maria van Diemen, the northernmost point on New Zealand's mainland. Soon we were dead in the water. The
fog thickened to leave a visibility of about twenty-five
yards. Then I thought I heard a foghorn! Next I thought
there was a distant throbbing pulse in the fog astern. I
dismissed the sound; surely it was my heart beating. Suddenly it came again, closer now! The throbbing now
sounded like a ship with its prop out of the water, soft-
ened by distance and fog. I ordered Bri to cease her
chatter and listened intently. It was closing at twenty
knots, and visibility was practically zero. *Sea Lion* had no
radar reflector. The time was 1900 Greenwich. That ominous hooting whistle was distinct by now, briefly drown-
ing out the pulsing throb of engine and screw. I swung
the tiller from side to side. We had steerage, but barely.
I scrambled to the cabin top with the dishpan lid and
held it aloft in hand. The lid was about eighteen inches
in diameter. I focused the concave directly at the oncom-
ing sounds. The ship was on our course and coming right
down the keel line! I ordered Bri below to ensure a clear
path to the tiller and remained holding the dishpan lid

aloft. Now the hooter was so loud it shook my rib cage. I strained to see astern, watching the water for the first sign of movement. The *hoot* came more in my right ear than the left. The next *hoot* confirmed that the ship had changed course! Suddenly white water came rolling up out of the fog. I dropped the pan lid and dived for the tiller, put it hard to weather, and waited. *Sea Lion* answered lazily, but in time to catch the roller square on her stern. It was the ship's starboard bow wave. The ship passed at fifteen knots. By leaning over the gunwale I could see the bow stem outline only a few feet above its billowing wake. Then props slapping the water to a froth astern. It passed at about one hundred yards. It was high in the water, its superstructure obscured in fog. It went on hooting into the soft gray distance. I looked below; Bri was asleep. The time was 1922 Greenwich.

I released the tiller, and *Sea Lion* came back on course as though nothing had happened.

No telling how much time passed, but the fog was thinning some when another vessel came bobbing and rolling up out of the south. Apparently it was a fishing vessel, about fifty feet and beamy. As it drew closer, I could see five men in foul-weather gear lining the rail. The wind had moved a bit north and freshened some. *Sea Lion* was sliding along in the fog at three knots with a free helm. The vessel had a handsome pilothouse of varnished wood. By her rigging she was a lobster boat; her life ring read "PANDORA." She would pass astern. As *Pandora* crossed our wake, she came about to come along the weather side. I was anxious about having another vessel so close till I saw their faces. They were seamen. *Pandora* stayed with her bow just aft of *Sea Lion*'s beam.

"Hello. We picked you up on radar. Thought you were one of us!"

"No. We're *Sea Lion,* nineteen days out of Brisbane."

"Anything you need? Petrol?"

"No, no engine. What's the range to Reinga Light?"

One of them ducked back in the pilothouse with the helmsman. Bri woke at voices and came up the ladder. Those fishermen on the rail broke into grins. "How many aboard there?"

"Me and the mate here."

The one in the pilothouse ducked back out. "Hold your heading. Eight miles."

"Thanks."

"What's your home port?"

"Los Angeles."

*Pandora* pulled away to weather and black diesel smoke poured out of her stack. The wind was freshening as fog lifted.

We almost passed Reinga Light without seeing land. It slipped by in the haze three miles to starboard. I saw other lobster boats off to port. From their angle of heel, they were hauling pots. The wind was freshening out of the northwest. By the time we were halfway between Reinga and North Cape Light the wind was approaching gale. All the lobster boats were at flank speed on our course, for North Cape. One, *Producer* as I recall, was passing us a short distance to weather. That vessel was pitching and rolling something fierce. When one of the fishermen ventured on deck, he was forced to hold to a lifeline and knotted ropes hanging from the racks aft. I sat at the tiller drinking a cup of coffee in perfect comfort. The lobsterman was doing less than eight knots; we were doing more than six. I couldn't help but feel that the beating they were taking wasn't worth a knot and a half.

Soon it was necessary to tuck another reef in the main and strike the staysail. It was late afternoon and blowing a full gale as we approached North Cape, and dark by the time we rounded the point. I could see the lights of fishing boats all in a row. They appeared to be very close

in to the shore. Though we were in the lee of a cliff some two hundred feet high, that gale was pouring over with tremendous force. As *Sea Lion* drew deeper into the lee, cat's-paws and dead spots caught her. One minute we were knocked down, the next screaming toward shore with all sheets in hand. The yankee jib sheet got loose; let her go. We fought and clawed our way toward shore till it seemed the bowsprit was in bushes. I dashed forward and let go the anchor, throwing off all halyards on the way back to the cockpit. I was on the verge of fainting from fatigue. The lights of one fishing boat were to starboard, the rest to port. They were comforting. *Sea Lion* was on cabin reaches on the anchor line. It held. I crashed below.

The next morning about nine Bri was hollering at me. She came down in the cabin. I woke up, sort of. "Papa, Papa! There's a boat hanging over us! Come see!" I stumbled half conscious up the ladder. Sure enough, the bow of a fishing boat was hanging over the cockpit! A red-faced man wore a grin and held a live lobster in his hand. "Good morning to you! Thought you might like some fresh meat."

At first I was more concerned that the other vessel might stave in the taffrail. *Sea Lion* was yawing around on the anchor line, but the man at the wheel kept his stem an even foot from her port side! "Sure! Just drop it in the cockpit." It looked big enough to take my arm off! He let it go and the critter flapped about.

"Anything you need?"

"Sure would like some greens."

"I'll see what we can do."

The helmsman backed down and turned back for his anchorage. The vessel's name was *Protron,* out of Auckland.

By the time that lobster was in a tow sack hanging in the water, the sun came out. It was still blowing a full gale

and its force hit the water some hundred yards to our stern. There was a line of instant whitecaps! After break-fast we aired bedding and took a hot fresh-water bath. Just as we had finished, the trawler *Producer* came along-side with fresh butter, a chunk of meat, and a weather forecast; gale out of the northwest. We had a nice chat as I kept one eye out for *Producer*'s bow stem. These New Zealand seamen were impressive boat handlers. None of them would come aboard nor accept anything from *Sea Lion*. Regulations, they said.

"Anything you need, just let us know."

"Would you happen to know where we could haul out cheap?"

There was a consultation with the helmsman and more on the radio. "Bay of Islands. They got some sticks in the mud around Matavi Bay."

"Would you happen to have an extra chart for those waters?"

"We'll find you one."

They returned to anchor in the lee of that beautiful cliff.

The rest of that day Bri and I just lay around drying out, resting, and reading *Scuppers, the Sailor Dog,* while the five fishing boats visited amongst themselves. We went to bed at dark in dry bunks while the gale howled high overhead.

Early the next morning, right after breakfast, the trawler *Wiaona* dropped by on its way home to Auckland. They were going in, "gale or no." The crew lowered a bucket full of soda pop and beer into the cockpit. They also gave us a dead fish to cut up for bait. We were living off the fat of the land in company with brave and accom-plished men.

Hardly had *Wiaona* departed when *Pandora* came alongside. To Bri they were old friends. She jabbered constantly, holding intelligent conversation with three

grown seamen at a time. They had charts for us. One of this coast and one of the Bay of Islands.

"They're old charts, mate. Don't pay much mind to the lights, but the shore ain't changed."

All in all, we had a lovely chat with the skipper and crew of *Pandora*. Many promises were made to meet later, but of course we haven't seen each other since.

Five hours later *Producer,* the one who'd brought us butter and meat yesterday, fell by with fresh turnip greens! One of the deckhands of another vessel had pulled them from his garden at home and they hadn't been used. They were a little ragged, but they were sure enough greens! At no time on the voyage were my spirits higher than just now! Then they lowered aboard canned peaches and pears! They also had a weather forecast; gale out of the northwest. Frankly, I wished it could have gone on a lot longer, but it didn't.

Early the next morning, that of October 20, we hauled the anchor in light airs and headed southeast for the Bay of Islands.

*Sea Lion* was ghosting along under full sail when the trawler *Lorina* came alongside with a live lobster and barley sugar for the mate. They welcomed us to New Zealand and wished us a long stay.

The shoreline of North Island is magnificent in its isolation. One sees no sign of human habitation. Mysterious names such as Karikari, Whangaroa, Cavalli. It was early spring down here. By nightfall it was raining lightly, and we were beating into gentle easterly breezes. No sleep. In the lightly rainy dawn we came close to hitting a rock west of Cape Karikari. Two hours later the wind swung to north with authority. We were flying on under full sail! We passed mile after mile of pastoral beauty; not a road, house, or utility pole could be seen, only white dots of sheep and dark green timberland shrouded in wispy clouds. The water was so blue and clean as to

seem virgin. Flying fish and seabirds of every description
cavorted about us. Surely we were returning "home"!

Soon it was blowing another gale out of the north. We
were too close to a lee shore to attempt reefing. Fatigue
and I studied the chart. There, up ahead—that must be
the entrance to the Bay of Islands. We went in. It wasn't.
*Sea Lion* was taking the whole gale dead astern under full
sail! The Cavalli are a group of islands off the coast.
Under normal conditions, as when ashore, they are extremely beautiful. The passage inshore around them is
studded with large rocks, but somehow we missed them,
and *Sea Lion* found herself in the lee! I three-reefed the
main and struck the staysail. Away we roared for the Bay
of Islands, in a full gale with a lee shore. All the rest of
that day we flew past matchless shoreline in the company
of great flocks of seabirds. Past the Needles! Then came
the big rock jutting up out of the sea, marking the entrance to the Bay of Islands. We turned downwind and
went roaring in as darkness fell.

With the fading light, wind abated. There were lights
ahead. The wind continued to fall. Soon we were ghosting about with lights of settlements on both sides, five
miles off. I heard surf and dropped the anchor. Bri was
already asleep.

# Chapter Fifteen

I AWAKENED THE NEXT MORNING to Bri's chirping and a ferryboat passing close astern. There were small islands all about, and white water was breaking where our anchor lay. It's called luck.

The day broke fair, and I was in no hurry. We were not out on the terrible Tasman now. The ferryboat passed several more times while we had breakfast. They were close enough to hail and they pointed out the quarantine anchorage near the town of Paihia. Near noon I hauled the anchor and fiddled our way over there. With the anchor down in the indicated spot, I scrambled aloft with the foul-weather jacket, the only thing yellow aboard for a "Q" flag. With it secured to the port shrouds, we waited.

Shortly before noon two men in business suits appeared on dock ashore. They motioned for us to come alongside. With the anchor aboard, *Sea Lion* nudged up to the dock under staysail alone.

Both the men were young, one the doctor, the other customs. They were friendly, even seemed to be expecting us, and barely flinched when I handed them our passport covers. The numbers were perforated in the covers, but I didn't know which was mine and which Bri's. It didn't seem to matter to them. Their only concern or interest was canned meat. We had none. We were cleared, and they left wishing us a pleasant stay, after pointing out the pub over across the bay in the town of Russell.

I was straightening up the lines, preparing to cast off the dock, when I noticed a man standing there. He wore shorts on bowed legs and a tam on his head. In a heavy Scottish brogue he asked where we were from. When I told him Los Angeles, his face lit up. He too was from California, and his name was Alex Stuart. He adopted us when he discovered we were semi-singlehanding. When I asked if there was a laundromat, he said yes, over in Matavi Bay, but we should come straight with him to his house, meet his wife, Mickey, and wash our clothes there.

I didn't want to burden them; besides, my mind was on the pub. Promising to look them up, we sailed across the bay to Russell. The pub was in a nice old hotel. We anchored right in front of it, inflated the dinghy, and went ashore.

The bartender called me "Captain" and the beer was great. Bri had a Shirley Temple, and we were enjoying being ashore when I looked out toward *Sea Lion* just in time to see a trimaran ram her port side! It was apparent from his antics that the bearded man on the trimaran didn't know what he was doing. I hurried out in the dinghy while Bri played on the pebble beach. When I got on board, the man on the trimaran was clinging desperately to *Sea Lion*'s taffrail with one hand, trying to untangle his anchor line with the other. There was a V-shaped hole the size of my fist right through *Sea Lion*'s sheer strake amidships on the port side! I helped the fellow get his gear down, told him to forget it, and went back to finish my beer. This man, too, was an American.

As it turned out, the laundromat was a joke. Early the next morning we sailed back across the bay to Paihia and went ashore to find Alex Stuart. His wife, Mickey, was a delight. They put their house to our use and comfort. Bri now had an Aunt Mickey and an Uncle Alex. They were more than aunt and uncle to me.

It was November, and summer was coming on in New

Zealand. Everyone we met was friendly. The Bay of Islands became more beautiful by the day. *Sea Lion* had not
been hauled out for bottom inspection since we'd run
across that sandstone bar back in Gladstone, Australia.
She needed a new Vane Jane. I found the "sticks" those
lobster fishermen had told me about around behind the
town of Russell in a bay called Matavi. They were nothing more than tea-tree poles stuck in the mud, but the
incline was just right for a straight keel, and there was a
seven-foot tide. Zane Grey's old boat was there, being
fitted out and painted for the coming game fishing sea-
son.

Bri was ashore with her "Auntie" Mickey. Proper arrangements had been made with the "owner" of one of
those spaces between the sticks, and *Sea Lion* and I came
smartly into Matavi Bay with a beam wind. Alex was
ashore with a skiff and line. The plan had been to anchor,
secure the line from shore, and pull *Sea Lion* into the
space at high tide. We had tarried too long at the pub;
the tide was in now. I dropped the main. There were
seamen and some salty Maoris there ashore. I pointed
*Sea Lion* toward the space and struck the yankee jib. With
the staysail sheet in hand, we slid neatly between the
poles, inches to spare on both sides, just enough fetch to
snug her keel in the mud for a gentle stop. Everyone was
impressed, including myself. When the tide went out, *Sea
Lion* was high and dry. The haul-out was free.

There was no serious damage from the sandstone bar.
The new vane would be easily fabricated, but she'd never
be Vane Jane. That hole in the sheer strake was puttied
in. Fat shellfish called cockles could be picked out of the
mud at low tide by the bucketful. They were delicious
steamed in their own juice with a bit of garlic. Illegal
oysters grew on the rocks. I had my first contact with the
native Maori.

*Sea Lion* was patched up and back in the water before

Boxing Day. That day signals a three-week vacation for *all* New Zealanders. Ah, summertime in the Bay of Islands! Sailboats of every description poured into the bay daily. The anchorage off the pub at Russell was a forest of masts. Once lonely beaches on uninhabited islands were now packed. By then Bri had friends on both sides of the bay and spent only about a third of her time aboard *Sea Lion.* When she was aboard, our favorite hangout was an old hotel on an outer island. We had first found it because its water had been recommended as the sweetest and best-keeping. The place had once been the center of communication for the outlying islands. The main stop for the milk run. It was still the only island with a telephone and post office. Just before the holidays it had been a quiet retreat, but now it bustled with New Zealand tourists. A Grumman Widgeon seaplane landed daily and taxied up out of the tiny bay onto the beach. They were remarkable little seaplanes with daredevil pilots who put on a good show with every landing and takeoff. A vital link in the country's public transportation.

One of the women working in the dining room let her guard down for a moment and Bri grabbed her heart. They hung out together, and I started putting a garden in the old abandoned plot behind the hotel. The lady was interested in having a big garden but had only a few things for the table. I worked at it whenever *Sea Lion* was in the little bay.

When Bri wasn't aboard, I sailed alone among the islands. It was a sailor's paradise—never too far from a pub. Everyone in New Zealand either has a boat or is kin to one who does. I was rapidly coming to respect their boat handling. Sailboats were by far the most numerous. By this time I had fitted *Sea Lion* with a pair of nine-foot sweeps. Fold-down oarlocks were secured on one-inch cockpit coaming. They were handy when there was no

wind, which was rare. In the first month at the Bay of
Islands I learned more about sailing *Sea Lion* than I did
in the crossing. We really had it down. Soon I knew the
holding qualities and habits of the anchorages. Her sails
still didn't fit properly, though I'd had the main recut at
the gaff, but we made do. It was great fun to come flying
into a crowded anchorage, pick a spot, sprint forward
and drop the anchor, let it run as long as possible before
hitting another boat or the pier, snub off, and jump to
throw the halyards off as she hit the end of warp and
swapped ends. There's no other way if you don't have an
engine and the wind is blowing.

Occasionally, even in the summer, the Bay of Islands
would have eighty-knot gales. Then everybody scrambled to get into Matavi, which was in the lee of prevailing
storms. It's not a large bay, and has only six to eleven feet
of water, but the black clay bottom allows a short scope.
Several hundred boats would come into that bay, ride
out the blow, then depart without ever scratching paint
or raising voices. I was impressed.

In one such stay at Matavi I met a young man off an
aluminum motor sailer. An American named Don Boots,
he had sailed from California with his parents and two
brothers. Don was a bright lad and a good hand. One day
he and I took *Sea Lion* up the Kerikeri. It's a winding little
tidal river that ends in a basin at an old stone mill. A
beautiful spot but a mean piece of sailing to get in and
out. About three days in all.

All too soon the holidays were ending. No more boat
parties and cooking on the beach. All the sailboats left,
all but five or six, the ones who'd been there before it had
all started on Boxing Day.

It was getting harder to get Bri to come aboard, even
to spend one night. It was okay when there were parties,
but she much preferred the attention ashore. The one
place she did like to go was back out to the island hotel.

The land was beginning to get a hold on me too. I looked for five acres. I found several. Five acres was all a foreigner, especially an American, was allowed to own. Of course I didn't have enough money, and investigated selling *Sea Lion*. It nearly broke Don Boots' heart. Weeks went by in the turmoil of what to do. There was the problem of the considerable duty to be added to the price of the vessel. The one serious buyer would never take her to sea again. I was tired. *Sea Lion* was becoming run down as I spent less time aboard and more in the pubs ashore. I began to sense that the Bay of Islands was a long way from where anything was happening. There was no way for me to make a living there—perhaps an existence, but hardly a living. I got a bad infection on my foot from the garden soil. In what I thought was the end, economics made the decision for me. There was not enough money to live ashore, but there was enough to outfit for a passage to Santiago, Chile.

After waiting a week for favorable wind, Bri and I sailed for Auckland to be closer to supplies. I was expecting an overnight romp down the coast. No sooner had *Sea Lion* stuck her nose out of the Bay of Islands than the wind pulled around to blow on her bow. And I mean blow! We were forced to seek shelter just around the headland in Wangamumu Harbor. It was an old abandoned whaling station, and one of the locations where I'd found a piece of dirt. Part of the old pier was still there, and the rusted boiler and concrete vats for melting down blubber. It was a good anchorage with the wind howling outside. There was another vessel there, a sloop, with a man and his wife from Auckland, late on their way back from the holidays. It was a pleasant stay waiting with them for a following wind. After a day and night he decided to try it with engine assist.

The wind was dying, and next day it came favorable out of the north. We hauled anchor and sailed on a fine quartering wind—for about an hour. Then it hauled

around and came right down the bow! We fought the whole day to shelter on Grand Island. After two more days we set out for Auckland and the wind came from there. I was getting the distinct impression that the sea had withdrawn our permission. The whole route down to Auckland is strewn with islands and headlands. We clawed our way from shelter to shelter, and always left with a favorable wind. It was becoming an epic voyage! At one point it had me so spooked I became seasick. Though I didn't throw up, the sick feeling was profound. The ride was so rough Bri complained of her kidneys.

Nine days after departing from the Bay of Islands we were still clawing our way past the Auckland waterfront to the yacht harbor. As soon as we were behind the breakwater, I dropped the anchor in total exhaustion. I think right then I'd had enough sailing to last me for a while. Bri didn't even have to think about it.

I found getting around Auckland from a sailboat very awkward. Occasionally the thought of roaring across the forties to South America got me moving. I went to the American consul to get us some new passports. We were treated with dignity, and the man had me raise my right hand and swear to defend the Constitution of the United States against all enemies, foreign and domestic.

It brought a change over me, or at least what I was thinking about.

I continued to provision in a halfhearted manner, but my bottom line became the need for a cook and dish-washer.

Since arriving in the Bay of Islands I had been on the lookout for such a person, so long as it was a young female. I'd tried to get to know one and quickly recalled past experiences. One day a young lady appeared on the dock in Auckland looking for passage on a sailboat. I told her that if she survived a trip back to the Bay of Islands she could have the job. Some deal.

*Sea Lion* wasn't ready, but that young lady was the most

important factor in the decision about when or whether we set out for South America. We waited for following winds. They came, just long enough to carry us past the Auckland waterfront.

It was tooth and nail the rest of the way, including a grounding and wait for tide change with *Sea Lion* standing on her keel, braced upright by the two nine-foot sweeps. Six days later I dropped anchor off the Russell pub, knowing for sure we no longer had permission.

Apparently that experience stretched the limits of the young lady's expectations. I rowed her ashore and never saw her again.

It was coming on winter, and the rains came. Don Boots and I braved it longer than most. Soon it was too hard for Bri to be aboard. Cold rain fell constantly for weeks on end. Nights were getting cold and gales more than occasional. Everything became mildewed aboard. I rented a room ashore, and it too was mildewed. The rain seemed never to let up, sometimes more than an inch an hour.

One day, when it was only blowing mists, Don and I were out on the Russell pier. "Don, I'm gonna give you *Sea Lion.*" At first he was simply delighted! He was a good navigator, a fine seaman, and he wanted to go to sea in his own vessel. Also he was eighteen.

After a day he began to wonder about strings attached to the vessel. I told him that a condition of the gift was that he should not sell *Sea Lion.* He, too, would have to find the right person to give her to. Bri was overjoyed.

After visiting his parents, who had become residents down in the city, Don said his father said he should get a receipt for "one dollar and good and valuable consideration," or some such, so we sat down and drew up one. Then we drew up another which said I had given the boat to him. We were having such a good time we even made a fresh logbook with an entry directing him to deliver the

vessel to me in Los Angeles, taking whatever course and time he deemed necessary. Then we took all the documents to be notarized.

I took the ferry over to Paihia to fetch Brief. The Widgeon was to leave from the Russell side, so we said our goodbyes to Alex and Mickey. I promised to keep in touch. We rode the ferry back in a driving rain. It rained hard all night.

Don, Briewfn, and I were on schedule the next morning. It was early, and nothing was open. We stood with the luggage in doorways to get out of the rain. *Sea Lion* was barely visible in the bay alone.

The Widgeon that was to take us to Auckland to catch a flight to Los Angeles was past due, but we couldn't blame the pilot for being late in these conditions. Presently there was a roar of feathered props out in the bay, and the Widgeon came taxiing out of the haze. In a frothing spray that must have blinded him almost totally, the pilot taxied up on pebble beach and spun the plane around. We ran with luggage to get under the wing just as it stopped. A passenger got off and ran for shelter.

The Widgeon could carry five passengers and luggage. Bri and I were the only ones boarding. With luggage loaded and our seat belts fastened, the pilot put the throttle to it and the seaplane waddled back into the water. He kept the throttle on and took off right out of the harbor. I sat facing forward with a window view under the port wing. He banked in a turn toward Auckland. Bri was across from me, grinning and holding the pink teddy.

The last time I saw *Sea Lion,* she was shrouded in mist two hundred feet below, bobbing on wake the Widgeon had left behind.